Nurturing Emotional Literacy

Nurturing Emotional Literacy

A Practical Guide for
chers, Parents, and those
the Caring Professions

Peter Sharp

David Fulton Publishers
London

David Fulton Publishers Ltd
Ormond House, 26–27 Boswell Street, London WC1N 3JZ

www.fultonpublishers.co.uk

First published in Great Britain by David Fulton Publishers 2001

Note: The right of Peter Sharp to be identified as the author of this work has been asserted by him in accordance with the Copyright, Designs and Patents Act 1988.

Copyright © Peter Sharp 2001
Reprinted 2001

British Library Cataloguing in Publication Data
A catalogue record for this book is available from the British Library

ISBN 1–85346–678–6

The publishers would like to thank Christine Avery for copy-editing and Sophie Cox for proof-reading this book.

Typeset by Elite Typesetting Techniques, Eastleigh, Hampshire
Printed in Great Britain by Bell and Bain Ltd, Glasgow

Contents

Emotional Literacy

People are able to recognise, understand handle, and appropriately express their emotions.

Become successful by managing your emotions

Peter Sharp

BSc PGCE DipEd CertEdPsych MA CPsychol

Never doubt that a small group of thoughtful, committed people can change the world. Indeed, it is the only thing that ever has.

Margaret Mead

To Lindsey, Chloe and Poppy

Keeping my feet firmly on the ground,
anchored rather than tethered.

Infinity buckets!

Acknowledgements

I am pleased and grateful to the many people who have contributed to what I feel and think about life, my early and formative years in Aberdeen, Scotland with my parents, brothers and sisters, grandparents, and aunties, uncles and cousins. Later friends and teachers became more influential, and later again colleagues both in schools and education authorities. My many trips to Israel were also important, and especially my friend Michal.

The most important and influential formal learning experience I have ever had was my experience at the Tavistock Clinic, tutorials with John Bowlby, the sapiential authority of Elsie Osborne, the skills of John Byng-Hall, the warmth and decency of Doris Liebowitz, the psychotherapy of Dilys Daws, and the energy of Emelia Dowling. I left the 'Tavi' with the advice: 'find a kindred spirit, form a dyad, and others will follow your enthusiasm.' It worked for me.

I have kept contact with friends from my teaching days in Langdon School, Newham and value greatly the friendships from my teaching days at Park High School, Harrow. Only some people can make sense of their own journeys in relation to their friends... so I'm pleased to still be seeing some of my pals from Harrow (The Burley, Jones, and Barnes families).

My early years as an educational psychologist, first as a locum EP in Luton and then ten happy years in Hampshire persuaded me to get writing. Since joining Southampton in 1997 things have really taken off... a combination of supportive elected members and especially June Bridle, leader of the council, and an enthusiastic and motivating director of education, Bob Hogg, resulted in emotional literacy embedding across the city. Other true friends and valued colleagues who have gone the extra mile in supporting me to make emotional literacy more than mere rhetoric are Peter Lewis, head of children and young people's services and Ian Sandbrook, chief inspector for Southampton. Inclusion in Southampton is developing well, and Ahmad Ramjhun, Education Officer SEN is a stalwart in making that happen.

Southampton Psychology Service is made up of a group of extraordinarily talented and hard-working people who earn my admiration and respect by making 'continuous improvement' a reality, while daily promoting emotional literacy. What we achieve together is astonishing, and I thank them all for going the extra mile and for their loyalty to our shared concern. Special warm thanks to Adrian Faupel and Liz Herrick my friends and co-authors on previous work.

Finally, my own balance (such as it is) is sustained by the astonishing tolerance and support of Lindsey, my wife, and the rawness and immediacy of the love of my children Chloe (12) and Poppy (10)... thank you for putting up with me.

I hope this book touches your life in a helpful and meaningful way... if it does tell me about it:

p.sharp@southampton.gov.uk

Chapter 1

What is Emotional Literacy?

People are hot,
People are cool,
Sometimes I'm bright,
Sometimes a fool.

People often laugh,
People often cry,
Sometimes I'm happy,
Sometimes painfully shy.

People can shrink,
People can grow,
Sometimes I'll be open,
Sometimes I just flow.

Feelings are powerful,
Thinking is too,
One without the other,
And who are you?

Introduction and definition

Emotional literacy may be defined as the ability to recognise, understand, handle, and appropriately express emotions. Put more simply, it means using your emotions to help yourself and others succeed.

An emotion is defined as a *disturbance of mind; a mental sensation or state; instinctive feeling as opposed to reason* (Concise Oxford Dictionary), and therein lies a dilemma. Given that feelings are not 'reasonable' then trying to read them, and hence become emotionally literate, may seem like an impossible task. However, the central purpose of this book is to show that emotional literacy can be nurtured despite being a process or journey without a final end-point or destination. Nurturing emotional literacy can be likened to learning to play a musical instrument: perfection is never attained, but you hope to reach a point when you like what you see and hear.

Perhaps some readers will have concerns about the use of the term *Emotional Literacy* on the grounds that strictly speaking you can't 'read and write' emotions. I have chosen to use the term *Emotional Literacy* in preference to the other interchangeable term found abundantly in the literature, namely *Emotional Intelligence,* for two reasons. Firstly, *intelligence* has accrued a pejorative connotation, which would undermine the positive message I hope to impart in this book, and, secondly, *intelligence* has frequently been seen as rather fixed or stable over time and we just know that people can change dramatically in terms of their emotional state and stability.

The term 'emotional intelligence' was first used by psychologists Peter Salovey and John Mayer in 1989, and though earlier work by other psychologists referred to there being different types of intelligence this appears to be the first instance linking the affective domain (emotions) and the cognitive domain (intelligence) in this way. A few years later Daniel Goleman, a journalist and former editor at *Psychology Today,* popularised the notion of emotional intelligence in a worldwide best-selling book that put forward the view that emotions pay a far greater role in thought, decision-making, and individual success than is commonly acknowledged.

Goleman said: 'We have gone too far in emphasising the value and import of the purely rational – what IQ measures – Intelligence can come to nothing when emotions hold sway.' Goleman's book *Emotional Intelligence* (1996) has sparked considerable interest, and here in Britain there have been parallel movements aiming to reassert the importance of the emotions particularly with regard to education, and as part of a drive towards a more inclusive society.

Claude Steiner coined the term 'emotional literacy' and used it in print in 1979 in his book *Healing Alcoholism.* He has since gone on to train people on a programme that is designed to develop emotional literacy skills. Steiner's work is important, particularly in a therapeutic and personal development setting, but this book seeks to consider emotional literacy at a systemic and organisational level as well as that of the individual.

In Chapter 3 we will return to the theme of developing our own emotional literacy, but now we'll consider the relevance of emotional literacy and why it is worth studying.

Why does it matter?

After a period of over-focus on valuing that which is easily measured, such as reading, spelling, and number ages, educators are, at last, rethinking how to measure other attributes that we value. Even more radically, we have to redefine precisely what is valued. So, for example, the Qualifications and Curriculum Authority (QCA) has been considering the curriculum implications of 'Preparation for Adult Life' via a working group, whose findings will have influence in this context.

Clearly 'literacy' and 'numeracy' *are* highly valued and need to be at the heart of our national education agenda to raise standards, but I believe that they should be *equal* partners with the promotion of 'emotional literacy'. Estelle Morris, when speaking as Under-Secretary of State for School Standards, said: 'Developing children as rounded people and active members of the community is at the heart of what schools are about.' The incorporation of the affective, cognitive, and physical domains at the heart of education policy means reinstating the concept of educating the 'whole child' rather than fragmenting their education into component parts. This is not a return to some 'hippy 60s revival', but rather a forward-looking attempt to apply the same rigour to overall individual and societal development that has been happening in isolated parts of our education system. Standards in literacy are clearly rising, and that can only be beneficial to individuals and society generally, but there is a paucity of evidence to show that we are making parallel gains in helping children to become positive and well-rounded citizens.

Emotional literacy, and hence emotional learning, matters most because it will enable children to achieve their best and to make a greater contribution to society. Susie Orbach, psychoanalyst and co-founder of Antidote (a national charity set up in 1995 to promote emotional literacy), argues that:

> Emotional development has been seen as unnecessary, as an extra that is just too hard to fit in given the constraints of the national curriculum, as already existing in Circle Time or Personal and Social Development, or as something that relates exclusively to children in difficulty.

Orbach goes on to assert the need for a vision of an emotionally literate people, if we are to achieve a robust and emotionally literate society.

Arguably the key to promoting emotional literacy is to raise self-esteem; this was recognised well before Goleman's book, and led to the establishment of the national Self-Esteem Network in England in 1992 with an aim of promoting self-esteem in policy and practice. The original Self-Esteem Directory lists many of the organisations and individuals active in this work (including the author and colleagues listed as Southampton Psychology Service), and demonstrates that this work is not new but rather a reframe of earlier ideas.

Essentially, emotional literacy matters because:

1. We need to *recognise* our emotions in order to label or define them.
2. We need to *understand* our emotions in order to be effective learners.
3. We need to *handle (or manage)* our emotions in order to develop positive and wholesome relationships.
4. We need to *appropriately express* our emotions in order to develop as rounded people capable of helping ourselves, and so become emotionally healthy. In turn we will be better able to help others.

Kevin McCarthy, of *Re:membering Education* (a network of teachers and others seeking to develop all children's faculties and deepen the education debate) wrote a leaflet, with James Park and others, entitled, *Learning by Heart* published, widely in 1998 about the role of emotional education in raising school achievement. This was written in consultation with many 'stakeholder organisations' active in the promotion of emotional literacy, and McCarthy advances a rationale for why emotional learning matters:

(a) Understanding emotions is directly connected with motivation and with cognitive achievement;
(b) Dealing with emotions helps to develop better relationships and a sense of psychological and mental well-being;
(c) Emotionally developed young people are better equipped to live with difference;
(d) Our moral outlook and value systems are deeply shaped by our attitudes and feelings;
(e) Our sense of meaning and purpose is derived as much from feeling as from understanding.

James Park (Director of Antidote: The Campaign for Emotional Literacy), speaking at a conference of over 100 educational psychologists in 1999, said that the reasons why emotional literacy is important include:

• Positive emotions influence concentration, memory, problem-solving and learning skills.
• Positive relationships enable individuals to break out of dysfunctional patterns.
• Emotional literacy promotes creativity, innovation, and leadership.
• Emotional literacy has a measurable impact on the performance of organisations.

Taken together with the rationale outlined above it is clear that emotional literacy matters, and there is some urgency about setting a national agenda to promote and nurture our emotional literacy.

Developing the 'whole person' (adult or child) is likely to have demonstrable benefits for the individual and society by increasing people's capacity to contribute and achieve in terms of both productivity and personal development. Failure to pursue the goal of nurturing emotional literacy will result ultimately in poorer productivity and increased social exclusion.

John Bowlby (1987) said: 'Deprived children are the source of social infection as real and as serious as are carriers of diphtheria and typhoid.' While the term 'primary caregiver' was sometimes substituted for the word 'mother', Bowlby held to his views and said, aged 80: 'The very high incidence of mental ill-health, loneliness, suicide and depression: these are the fruits of inadequate care for children.' Bowlby was criticised for implying that mothers of young babies should not work, when in fact he simply asserted that babies need a stable and caring relationship with a parent or primary caregiver. Children's emotional literacy is dependent on an enduring and stable early years experience, and parents are more likely to provide this than paid carers.

There is compelling evidence that our emotional literacy or mental health is inextricably linked to that of our parents. In a study entitled *Mental Health and Adolescents in Great Britain (Stationery Office 2000)* involving 10,000 face to face interviews with children aged 5–15 years and 4,500 with young people aged 11–15 years and questionnaires to their teachers, one striking finding was the relationship between social class and mental health. 14% of children with mental disorders came from social class V (unskilled occupations) as compared to 5% of children from social class I (professional families). In addition, other factors were correlated with increased likelihood of childhood mental illness such as: parental employment (20% where parents unemployed, 8% where employed), lone parents twice as likely to have children with mental disorder as two parent families, parental qualifications (15% of those with no qualifications and 6% for parents who had been to university), parental mental health (47% of children with parents who had a mental health problem). Now while none of these correlations imply direct causation, it is more likely that emotionally literate parents will have emotionally literate children who will go on to be emotionally literate parents themselves.

Breaking into cycles of deprivation might better be achieved by promulgating virtuous circles, whereby parents, caregivers and teachers are supported in becoming more emotionally literate themselves, and as a consequence are better able to promote the emotional literacy of youngsters.

If a child is given insufficient emotional nurturance this can lead to poor mental health and ultimately can be life-threatening. Approximately one in four of us will have a mental health problem at some time in our life, requiring treatment or support from the caring professions, and what is most worrying is that this figure does not seem to be falling as overall living standards rise. While psychologists may argue about the relative contribution of nature and nurture in emotional development, there is convincing evidence that nurturing emotional literacy has beneficial effects, and the first three to five years are the most critical period for that to happen. That said, influence from parents and carers, siblings, relatives, teachers, peers, and other sources including the media, can all play a part in developing emotional literacy either to foster a good beginning or to ameliorate a poor early years experience.

In addition to promoting individual and societal emotional literacy for purely altruistic reasons, there is also a commercial and organisational imperative driving this work. Specifically, life success is clearly not solely mediated by cognitive intelligence but rather by a cocktail of multiple intelligences. Demetriou *et al.* (1998) describe how early theories of intelligence were termed *entity theories,* in that intelligence was seen as an internal, stable, and global 'trait', which could be assessed through performances but could not be changed. Later theories were *'incremental'*, in that they held that intelligence is composed of a number of different competences that can be developed through adequate training or experience: effort increases and, therefore, intelligence. Thorndike (in Atkinson *et al.* 2000), as early as the 1920s, talked of social intelligence and how learning occurs to promote this. Thorndike held that the learning of feelings and attitudes is mediated by *'solution learning'* that obeys the law of effect whereby instrumental response patterns or habits develop. So the idea of emotional intelligence is not at all new, though it took until 1989 for the term to be coined by Salovey and Mayer.

Higgs and Dulewicz (1999) suggest that there is general agreement that only 20 to 25 per cent of the variance in individual attainment and performance can be explained by differences in IQ. They also assert that the core proposition of the emotional intelligence 'school' is that *life success* requires a combination of an average level of 'traditional' intelligence with above average levels of 'emotional intelligence'. They go on to say that in attempting to explore the relationship between the concept of emotional intelligence and organisations the focus has been primarily on the individual's progress in the organisational context. However, there is clearly scope for examining how emotionally literate are organisations, as well as the individuals within them.

The competitive edge that may accrue from being a highly emotionally literate organisation is likely to drive some of this work forward for less than altruistic reasons. This is clearly an area of potential tension between those who seek to promote a more emotionally literate society and those who simply want to find 'factor X' that conveys commercial or competitive advantage in the market place. Perhaps emotionally literate competition is not a contradiction in terms… and we could have an emotionally literate market place?

In the next section we'll consider what emotions are and what functions they perform, in order to better understand how emotional literacy may be nurtured.

What are emotions?

Let us now turn to considering origins, theories, and approaches to emotions. A newborn baby has a very limited repertoire of emotions; basically there are two states: excitement or quiescence. Excitement manifests itself through crying, wriggling, rooting, or more violent movement. Some would argue that quiescence is not an emotional state at all, but is emotionally neutral. For those who believe this, babies have little expression of emotion, but others believe we come 'pre-programmed' with a set of emotions waiting to be developed. Certainly by late adolescence or early adulthood the same being will have developed a whole range of emotions, and their skill in recognising, understanding, handling, and appropriately expressing their emotions will depend to a large extent on environmental factors. These factors include parenting and care-giving, friendships (siblings and peers), education, and largely passive learning from media including television, films, print media and increasingly the world-wide web.

Emotional development is, however, a complex process that is interactional, involving 'temperament' (which is largely inherited) and environmental factors, such as those listed above. While 'emotions' and 'feelings' are used interchangeably in common parlance, it is important to note that 'feelings' are components or elements of 'emotions', but there is little agreement among authors about how emotions actually work. In the next section of this chapter some conflicting theories and views are described, but it is interesting to note that much of the theory around emotions is over 100 years old and yet still appears to have some contemporary validity.

Theories of emotions

Early theories of emotion include the work of Charles Darwin (1872), who was the first to assert that behaviour was the evolutionary product of a long ancestry. He proposed three principles governing emotion:

1. *The principle of associated habits.* This might include, for example, nostrils becoming flared during a fight, and so later flared nostrils became an expression of anger; similarly clenched fists become a symbol of anger or threat as a result of having been necessary for fighting.
2. *The principle of antithesis.* If hunching or crouching prepares us for a fight or flight, then its opposite – relaxed, open neck, fawning, extending a hand – suggests the opposite emotion.
3. *The principle of direct action of the nervous system.* Darwin thought that some behaviours, such as thrashing about in pain, had little meaning beyond an expression of an intense and widespread physiological response. In contemporary thinking this might be considered *arousal* or *activation.*

Evolutionary principles still have significance in any theory of emotion, and it is important then to remember that there is something very primitive about emotion. Clearly emotions have adaptive significance, and that holds true whether we live in a cognitively over-focused industrial society or one of the now very rare 'undeveloped' societies.

Theories of emotions try to explain the relationship between factual events or stimuli and subjective emotional experiences. Clearly the same event or stimulus may result in very different emotional experiences from person to person, precisely because we bring subjective interpretation to bear on processing each experience.

Emotions are complex and multi-layered and made up of four integral components according to Gross and McIlveen (1998); *Subjective feelings, cognitive processes, physiological arousal, and behavioural reactions.* The way these components interact and the relative weighting given to each of these distinguish different approaches and theories of emotions. The following discussion, more fully unpacked by Gross and McIlveen (1998), centres on two theories which give weight to the importance of physiological factors and two approaches (Schachter 1964, and Lazarus 1982) that highlight cognitive processes as important determinants of emotional experience.

The James-Lange theory of emotions is probably the earliest published theory of human emotion, and was described by William James in 1890. They proposed that emotional experience is the result, not the cause, of bodily and behavioural changes. Their counter-intuitive theory describes emotions as a by-product of automatic physiological and behavioural responses.

Cannon (1927) highlighted difficulties with this theory by arguing firstly that each emotion would require a specific pattern of activity to make it possible for each emotion to be experienced. Cannon's first criticism is supported by the work of Wolf and Wolff (1947) and Mandler (1962) that describes how different people may display different patterns of physiological activity when experiencing the same emotion, and it may even vary with the same person experiencing the same emotion on different occasions. There is some evidence to support the James-Lange theory as Ax (1953) and Schwartz *et al.* (1981) showed that emotions including fear, anger, happiness, and sadness are different in terms of heart rate, body temperature, muscular activity in the face, blood pressure and neural activity in the frontal lobes.

Cannon's second criticism was that physiological changes themselves do not produce changes in emotional states, and this is supported by the fact that people injected with adrenaline reported either no change in emotional state, or described a hypothetical 'as if' emotion.

Cannon's third criticism is that separation of the viscera from the central nervous system does not result in absence of emotional experience, whereas the James-Lange theory would assert that it does. The evidence from animal experiments generally supports Cannon's criticism, but some writers believe that it is inconclusive. So it is interesting to note that the James-Lange theory still appears to have some validity over 110 years after its publication.

The Cannon-Bard thalamic theory of emotion says that all emotions produce the same pattern of responses that correspond to the *fight or flight* response that prepares us for danger or emergency. Information is sent to the cortex and produces the sensations of emotion at the same time as physiological and behavioural responses are produced. So, the experience of emotion neither causes nor is the result of physiological and behavioural responses. Rather, physiological and behavioural responses occur as a result of an emotion-provoking stimulus and not the experience of emotion it produces. Later work shows that Cannon was almost certainly wrong in ascribing a central role to the thalamus, and is also wrong in suggesting that physiological and bodily activity play no role in emotion. Cannon was right, however, to assert that the brain plays a central role in emotional responses.

Schachter's two process theory of emotion (1964) postulates that emotional experience depends on two factors; firstly, physiological arousal occurs in the autonomic nervous system (and so is not under our control) and secondly, there is a cognitive appraisal (or interpretation) of the physiological arousal. For Schachter arousal still precedes emotional experience, as for James-Lange, but this is not sufficient to account for the emotional experience. Schachter argues that the degree of arousal determines an emotion's intensity, but only if a cognitive interpretation is made. In other words, the emotion experienced is ascribed meaning through cognitive processes. According to Gross and McIlveen, Schachter's influential theory has been described as a 'juke box' theory of emotion in which arousal is the coin we put into the juke box and cognition is the button we press to select an 'emotional tune'. However, there are critics of Schachter's work, including Hilgard *et al.* (1979), who document a number of concerns including the fact that later attempts to replicate Schachter's work have not upheld his findings.

The more recent work of Lazarus (1982) argues that cognitive processing is an essential prerequisite for the experience of emotion. Lazarus argues that primitive emotional responses (such as fear) might not involve any conscious processing, but do involve rapid and unconscious appraisal. In his theory people must comprehend, even if only in the form of a primitive evaluative perception, before they can experience emotion. Other writers, such as Eysenck and Keane (1990) assert that Lazarus's studies have direct relevance to everyday emotional experiences, and that there are some grounds for assuming that cognitive processes precede emotional experience.

What we can conclude from the above discussion is that there is no theory of emotion that enjoys universal acceptance, though interactionist perspectives appear to enjoy greater currency at present. Ethical constraints prevent us from inducing powerful emotive states in controlled settings, so it is likely that a comprehensive theory of emotions is still a long way off. What we can say is that basic emotions have evolutionary significance, and it may be that the ability to manage our emotions effectively in a variety of settings could have even greater significance in the 'information age'. Implicit in the belief that development of emotional literacy is possible, is the view that elements of cognition must come into play in the more effective management and expression of emotions.

How do emotions make life worth living?

A truly rounded human experience involves a diverse range of emotions, experienced at differing levels of intensity and stretching from subtle shades and nuance of feeling through to moments of ecstasy and agony. It's a perplexing paradox that we can have little understanding of happiness unless we also know unhappiness or sadness, and that our ability to love is tangled up with our experience of hate.

If we examine our emotional repertoire by considering just a few emotions then it will become clear how emotions do make life worth living. The Latin root of emotion is *movere* meaning 'to move', and the addition of '*e*' means to disturb or move away. By implication then, emotions cause us 'to move' and imply action, or at least a preparation for action. By contrast the word 'feel' is derived from Old English *felan;* related to Old High German *fuolen,* Old Norse *falma* meaning to grope, or the Latin *palma* to palm. So feelings are perceptions based on sensations, while emotions are predispositions to action.

Some emotions, such as *anger*, are widely regarded as negative. However, Faupel *et al.* (1998) see anger as a secondary emotion, and a reflection of emotional difficulties. So rather than being seen as negative, anger is seen as an essential part of being human, having evolutionary and adaptive significance, and being either useful and positive or harmful and negative. So how may anger help to make life worth living? Well, if we're able to channel our anger in useful ways then we may be able to prevent or correct injustices, support or save others in distress or danger, or simply use our anger to assert our right to get our needs met without violating the best interests of others.

Similarly the primary emotion of *fear* is often considered a distress state, but is life preserving as soon as we're able to move, and goes on conferring advantage provided we're not overexposed to fear-inducing events. Perversely, fear is a strong motivator, and actually sought by many and not just in recreational pursuits (e.g. 'roller-coasters' or thrill rides, sports involving speed and/or risk), but also in potentially life-threatening situations (e.g. driving on the public highway). However, no one doubts the near ecstasy induced in many children at fun fairs on increasingly daring rides. Similar visceral pleasure can be induced by plucking up the courage to risk asking out someone you've admired, while bearing the fear of rejection. Again then, *fear* may be useful and positive, or harmful and negative.

Happiness (or enjoyment) is an emotion that causes inhibition of negative feelings; it energises people and causes considerable physical changes (e.g. ranging from rolling around in laughter, even to the point of tears of joy, to gentle mirth or a wry smile).

Sadness (or sorrow) is a secondary emotion based on a loss, and may be real, anticipated, or imaginary. The loss may be related to various and very different constructs including people, relationships, status, face, or objects. Oddly, a degree of sadness can be considered pleasurable, as for example with a fond memory or as induced by some kinds of music, but the sadness of raw and immediate loss or bereavement is felt to be entirely painful.

Surprise (or wonder) is an adaptation to a more basic physiological startle response, and like other emotions it is bipolar: there being good and bad surprises.

Shame (or guilt) are generally inhibitors to actions and can lead to stultifying paralysis, whereas *remorse* more frequently leads to compensatory action.

Disgust (or aversion) is also an adaptation to a more physiological or visceral response, such as experienced with tainted, poisonous or offensive food or odours. At that basic level it may be a primary emotion, and clearly has adaptive significance, but generally is taken to be a secondary emotion. Some authors link *hate* to *disgust*, but it is unclear whether or not it is a separate emotion.

Finally we come to the most discussed emotion: *Love*. Love is a complex emotion, at its basic level concerned with sexual satisfaction or procreation, but at a higher order centred on deep friendship or caring without sexual connotations. Poets, painters, writers, musicians all end up describing emotions and the most commonly occurring of these is love. For most people the giving and receiving of love is sufficient to make life worth living, and yet we receive negligible formal training or education to understand, much less express, love well. A core element in nurturing emotional literacy is about learning to love yourself sufficiently to give and receive love.

Later in the book we look at developing a feelings vocabulary for children whether we are in role as a teacher, parent or carer, but all the words relating to feelings and emotions can be subsumed under those given above. There is no standard taxonomy of emotions, though some psycho-biologists tend to hold that all emotions are adjuncts to primal drives: hunger, fear, shelter and sex. There is also considerable debate about the blurring between emotions, feelings, temperament, and mood... all of which are related to affective states.

Summary of Chapter 1: What is Emotional Literacy?

Emotional Literacy: *the ability to recognise, understand, handle and appropriately express emotions.*
Emotional Literacy matters most because it will enable children to achieve their best and to make a greater contribution to society.

- We need to *understand* our emotions in order to be effective learners.
- We need to *manage* our emotions in order to develop positive and wholesome relationships.
- We need to *appropriately express* our emotions in order to develop as rounded people capable of helping ourselves, and so to become emotionally healthy. In turn we will be better able to help others.

Life Success requires a combination of an average level of 'traditional' intelligence with above average levels of 'emotional intelligence'.

Emotions are made up of *subjective feelings, cognitive processes, physiological arousal, and behavioural reactions.*

Theories of Emotions conflict with each other, but it is likely that cognitive processing occurs as part of the experience of emotion.

Emotions have evolutionary and adaptive significance, and may become increasingly important in determining our short-term, and even possibly long-term, success.

All you need is Love...   John Lennon

Action

For the reader: Note down what you think emotional literacy means to you. Before you read on, note too what you think you can do to promote your own emotional literacy.

For groups of adults: Describe (a) Someone you consider to be highly emotionally literate (characteristics, evidence, etc.) (b) Someone you consider to be emotionally illiterate (characteristics, evidence, etc.).

For teachers, carers or groups of parents: If children learn better from good role models than by formal teaching, what should they see from you? Make (a) *a dream* and (b) *a nightmare* list of characteristics of a model teacher, carer, or parent.

Chapter 2

Checking out your Emotional Literacy

SATOR
AREP0
TENET
OPERA
ROTAS

The Creator unmoving holds his creations in vortices.

Nurturing emotional literacy begins with *you*. When we have considered and worked on our own emotional literacy then we will be better able to nurture the emotional literacy of others.

This chapter describes the need for a personal audit of emotional literacy, acknowledges the hierarchy of human needs, and then goes on to explain how to undertake a comprehensive personal audit. This leads into Chapter 3 which unpacks ideas about how we can all nurture our own emotional literacy.

In the early 1940s Abraham Maslow elaborated a *hierarchy of human needs,* in which he saw progression from one level to another as being possible only when one's needs had been met at a lower level. The hierarchy may be summarised thus:

- Physiological needs – whereby basic needs such as food, rest, and shelter are met.
- Safety needs – whereby imminent threat or danger is avoided, and one feels sufficiently secure to explore and move on to meet other needs.
- Social, affiliation, and belongingness needs – whereby one develops group identity, becomes better able to express oneself and forms enduring friendships involving empathy.
- Self-esteem needs – whereby personal autonomy is fostered along with high levels of self-respect, self-confidence and a belief in one's ability to succeed.
- Self-actualisation needs – whereby personal fulfilment is achieved through expression of talents, helping others, and accruing recognition and respect particularly of peers.

Broadly the hierarchy continues to hold true, and is widely quoted in both psychology and management texts. There is a parallel between Maslow's hierarchy and the development of emotional literacy, albeit that it is slightly staggered, (Table 2.1).

Maslow's Hierarchy of Human Needs:	Level of Emotional Literacy [EL]:
• **Self-actualisation**	> **Extremely High EL, and recognised by others**
• **Self-esteem**	> **High EL, self-aware and motivated**
• **Social/affiliation/belonging**	> **Medium EL, development of empathy, caring and self-awareness**
• **Safety needs**	> **Low EL, preoccupation with forming attachments and being secure**
• **Physiological needs**	> **Base level of EL, centred on *fight or flight* response**

Table 2.1 Hierarchy of Emotional Literacy

Assuming that basic physiological needs are met, then the individual can begin to focus on higher order needs. Similarly, if a child or adult feels secure and there is no imminent danger, then they will begin to explore higher order concerns that incorporate reflection, self-awareness and caring about others. This kind of caring transcends the basic provision of safety, security and sustenance, and is about consideration of feeling states and other people's emotions. Relating this back to the original definition of emotional literacy, it implies that we are moving from recognising and understanding emotions into handling them more effectively. If an individual has had a solid experience of this through their early years, and a Kleinian perspective would hold this to be critical between 0–6 years, then the next phase is characterised by increasing autonomy, high levels of self-respect and self-esteem and an ability to see the importance of this for others. Currently only a small proportion of our population will move on to what Maslow calls 'self-actualisation' where the individual is highly emotionally literate and is recognised by others as being so. In a more emotionally literate society that proportion will grow.

Given that emotional literacy is not stable over time, and may include a set of competencies that are amenable to change, then it is clear that we move through the hierarchy even on a daily basis, and our likelihood of ever developing higher levels of emotional literacy will be linked to parenting and education. There is clearly a close relationship between emotional literacy and mental health; a mentally healthy individual is someone who has high levels of emotional literacy. In the context of Maslow's hierarchy it is crucial to aim to create the conditions that allow people to feel sufficiently secure so they can become more emotionally literate, and yet many of today's pressures mitigate against this happening. Park (1999) said reasons why promoting emotional literacy is currently so important include:

- waves of initiatives and continuous change;
- heightened expectations (e.g. in education);
- increased social diversity;
- effect on parents of insecure, high-pressure workplace;
- legacy of social exclusion (and the drive for greater social inclusion).

So, having established 'why' and 'why now' let us now consider 'how' to begin a process of emotional literacy audit.

Taking Stock

Various aspects of our life make us what we are, and frequently we become over-focused on just one area, typically work, to the detriment of other areas. If we allow ourselves 'time to stand and stare' then it becomes immediately apparent which areas are suffering, but it is often very difficult to implement even the glaringly obvious changes we need to make, because we have become stuck in a loop with well-rehearsed and dysfunctional scripts. Figure 2.1 shows the key areas of life that we might look at when taking stock. Following that, there is a 'satisfaction rating map' that you may use to evaluate how you feel about your life, and particularly your 'work-life balance'. The same ratings may feel very different to each individual, and this tool is therefore intended for developmental use, and not for 'norm referencing' with others.

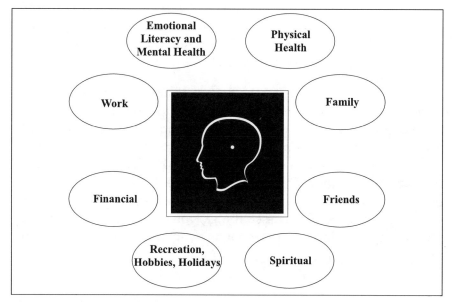

Figure 2.1   Areas of life

How you are doing in each of the areas above is open to subjective interpretation, so begin by giving yourself a satisfaction rating for each construct (1 = very low, 10 = very high):

1. **Emotional Literacy:**											
	1	2	3	4	5	6	7	8	9	10	
2. **Physical Health:**											
	1	2	3	4	5	6	7	8	9	10	
3. **Work:**											
	1	2	3	4	5	6	7	8	9	10	
4. **Family and/or partner:**											
	1	2	3	4	5	6	7	8	9	10	
5. **Friends:**											
	1	2	3	4	5	6	7	8	9	10	
6. **Spiritual:**											
	1	2	3	4	5	6	7	8	9	10	
7. **Financial:**											
	1	2	3	4	5	6	7	8	9	10	
8. **Recreation, hobbies, holidays:**											
	1	2	3	4	5	6	7	8	9	10	

Table 2.2   Areas of life – satisfaction rating map

Now that you've got a 'satisfaction balance sheet' you need to decide what needs changing, then begin to prioritise each of the development areas. If you live with someone or have family responsibilities then you may want to consider asking your *most significant other(s)* how they would rate you on the constructs above, and which ones they think need to change. (Your 'most significant other' may include a partner, friend, parent, sibling, or offspring). Having reflected and discussed things, you can make a contract with yourself by drawing up a personal development plan using the table over:

Personal Development Plan For:

Development area:	Rating on ____ (date)	Priority for change High/Med/Low	What I will do to change things:	Review date:
1. Emotional Literacy				
2. Physical Health				
3. Work				
4. Family and/or Partner				
5. Friends				
6. Spiritual				
7. Financial				
8. Recreation, Hobbies, Holidays				

Table 2.3   Personal development plan

When completing the column 'What I will do to change things', it is important to choose actions which are expressed in performance terms, which is to say that they should be *observable* and *measurable* (in terms of magnitude and/or frequency). What you write should pass the *Hey Mum or Hey Dad test*; e.g. *Hey Mum...* watch me get out on my bike two weekends out of four.

So, for example, alongside the heading emotional literacy, rather than put 'take more notice of how other people feel', have; 'check out/confirm other people's feelings when I'm unsure of them'.

We are more likely to commit to action if we make a contract with ourself and then share it with someone else, so plan to review how it goes with someone who will be trying to reinforce you for successive approximations to the explicit target. Given below are some examples of possible actions:

Development area:	Rating on 27th June (date)	Priority for change High/Med/Low	What I will do to change things:	Review date:
1. Emotional Literacy	7	M	> Check out/confirm other people's feelings when I'm unsure of them. >Ask people what a 'better-for-both' outcome would look like when we disagree about something.	27th July
2. Physical Health	6	M	> Get out on my bike at least 2 out of 4 weekends. > Swim with the kids once a month.	27th July
3. Work	9	M	> Go home twice a week by 6.00 and take no work home.	27th July

Table 2.4   Example of part of a completed Personal Development Plan

Having completed the 'Taking Stock' activities above, and with a short-term plan now in place, we can move on to take a 'helicopter view' of life.

This next activity was completed first with 14 psychologists and 10 school inspectors, as part of an introduction to emotional literacy over three years ago. Subsequently, this has been repeated with well over 2,100 people and has formed the basis of the introductory session on emotional literacy for over 400 head teachers, 1200 teachers, 200 psychologists and education officers, 100 parents, 150 governors and others from health and social services. This work has been undertaken by Southampton Psychology Service for staff from across the city, and as part of commissioned training or development consultancy with staff from 42 other local education authorities.

Few of us make time for reflection on our life, so try it now and see what happens!

My journey along life's highway

Guidelines for completing 'My Journey Along Life's Highway'

1. Start from when you were born, at the bottom of the sheet (See Appendix 2 for photocopiable blank pro-forma).
2. Put in all the milestones and events that you feel have been important in your life.
3. Include any achievements that you're pleased about, and some less happy experiences that have influenced you.
4. You can use words, images, dates, or symbols that help to tell the story of your journey so far.
5. On the back of the sheet:

*   Write a list of things you feel good about in your life.
*   Can you say why you do the job you do?
*   How might you answer the question: 'What is the most important thing life has taught me?'

6. If you feel it is appropriate, then share your work with someone.
7. In what ways can you help to nurture:

    (a) your emotional literacy
    (b) children's emotional literacy?

Below is a copy of my second go at doing this life map myself; I include this so you can get an idea of what a real attempt looks like. I hope to collect an anthology of these with a view to future publication. If you're willing to share your completed map, please send a copy to me, either anonymously or with some biographical data. Given below are my answers to the questions above:

Questions:	Answers (here's what I put)
What do you feel good about in your life?	❑ *My family, especially when we have time to enjoy things together. My love and my friendship with my wife.* ❑ *Being a dad. Seeing my children grow and change.* ❑ *My work… especially the variety and the enjoyment and encouragement that comes from working with some very talented and caring people.* ❑ *My health… because so far my body has been good to me.* ❑ *My car… 'cos it gives me no end of enjoyment. My bikes 'cos they're good for me.* ❑ *Getting the first book published… and now the third.*
Why do you do the job you do?	❑ *Because I genuinely feel I can touch other people's lives in a way that helps them (usually to help themselves), and I can learn from them too.*
What is the most important thing life has taught me?	❑ *I regularly remind myself that this really isn't a rehearsal and I need to try and enjoy the moment… the here and now. As someone said: 'focus on being not becoming.'*

Table 2.5 Answers to the questions on 'My Journey Along Life's Highway'

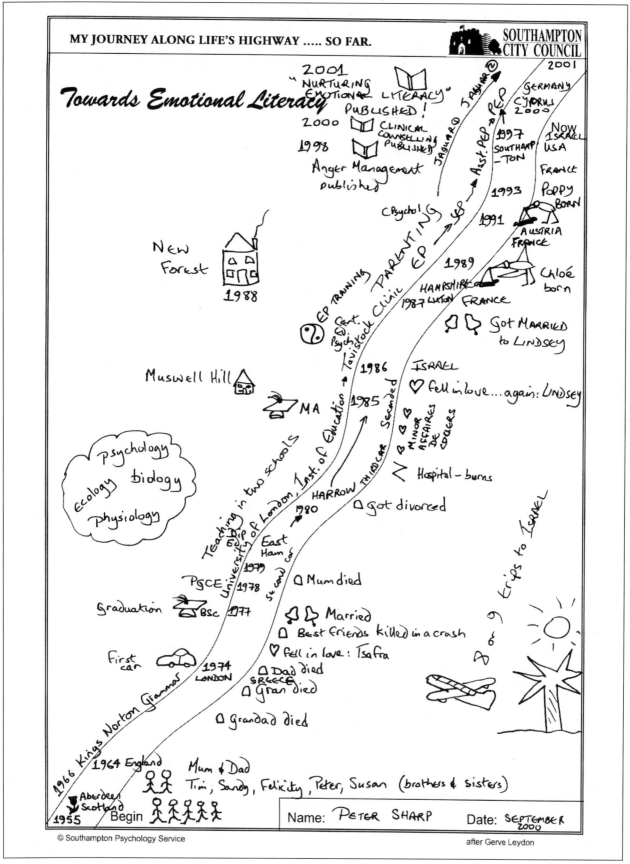

Figure 2.2 Life Map – 'My Journey Along Life's Highway' (See Appendix 2 for a photocopiable blank)

Where to next?

Combining the personal development plan and the life map will give the reader a comprehensive personal audit that allows a deeper insight into the options and priorities determining 'where to next'. The personal development plan demonstrates the degree to which life has become fragmented, perhaps with some areas dominating others in a harmful, unplanned and often unwanted way. The life map can show major milestones, influences, and timescales for your journey so far. So now you have a holistic overview of how emotionally literate you consider yourself to be, this will be complemented by a consideration of emotional competencies in Chapter 3.

Summary of Chapter 2: Checking out your Emotional Literacy

Emotional Literacy levels broadly correspond with Maslow's Hierarchy of Human Needs. Once basic needs are met (food, shelter, rest) and assuming individuals feel reasonably secure then they can begin to develop emotional literacy.

Early experience predicts later development of emotional literacy. Class, income, parenting, and family mental health are all correlated with children's mental health and emotional literacy.

Areas of Life include: emotional literacy, physical health, family, work, friendship, finance, recreation and spiritual development.

A *Satisfaction Rating Map* of the *Areas of Life* can be used to produce a *Personal Development Plan.* This plan can then be used to rectify perceived imbalances and promote an individual's emotional literacy.

Action

Complete the *Satisfaction Rating Map, Personal Development Plan,* and the *Life Map* as part of a comprehensive personal audit.

Together with your *most significant other* (e.g. partner, parent, etc.) or with a *learning partner* (e.g. a close trusted friend or colleague), share your work and set a review date.
Implement your *Personal Development Plan.*

Chapter 3

Nurturing your Emotional Literacy

The Highest reward for a person's toil is not what they get for it, but what they become by it.

John Ruskin

If emotional intelligence is taken to be a cluster of affective competencies or skills that determine how a person manages their own and other people's feelings; then emotional literacy is the process by which we develop those competencies and skills.

Skills, competencies or elements of Emotional Literacy

Authors disagree about what exactly the affective competencies are, though there is considerable overlap and similarity between them on which are core competencies.

Given in Table 3.1 is a summary of some of the main authors and the headings or elements they include in their descriptions of emotional intelligence. Before going on to describe how emotional literacy may be nurtured, it would be useful to unpack the skills, competencies or elements in Table 3.1 and to root them in worked examples.

Self-awareness

This is seen by many of the authors above as central to the development of emotional literacy. The skill or competence of self-awareness involves an incremental set of sub-skills; firstly, recognition of feelings requiring an extensive *feelings vocabulary*; secondly, an understanding of how those feelings impact on us; and thirdly, an ability to use that knowledge to manage the feelings effectively and to alter behaviour positively. Goleman (1996) describes the feeling of being 'flooded' or overwhelmed by feelings as an *emotional hijacking* and clearly the less self-aware you are the more likely to become 'hijacked'. If you're not sure how self-aware you are then you can monitor your self-awareness by keeping a diary for a while and doing a feelings check throughout the day. Label the feeling and rate it on a 10 point scale where 1 = weak or vague and 10 = very powerful.

Salovey and Mayer (1990)	Goleman (1996 and 1998)	Steiner (1997)	Higgs and Dulewicz (1999)
Self-awareness Managing emotions	Self-awareness Self-regulation	Knowing your own feelings Learning to manage our emotions	Self-awareness Emotional resilience Conscientiousness and Integrity
Motivating oneself	Motivation	–	Motivation
Recognising emotions in others	Empathy	Having a sense of empathy	Interpersonal sensitivity Influence Decisiveness
Handling relationships	Social Skills	Repairing Emotional Damage Putting it all together: emotional interactivity	(Interpersonal sensitivity)

Table 3.1   Skills, competencies, or elements of emotional literacy

Self-awareness: a worked example

Every Sunday evening a parent becomes apprehensive and anxious about having everything ready for the week… school uniforms, PE kit, their own work clothes, and the paperwork needed for Monday's meeting. The self-aware parent doesn't simply label this as Sunday evening blues, but analyses which bit causes the most anxiety and then commits to action to reduce or eliminate the unwanted feelings (e.g. getting the washing and ironing done routinely on Saturday and having the material for the meeting on Monday sorted by Friday, so that Sunday can be seen as a day off and enjoyed as relaxation and pleasure in being with the family. Alternatively the emotionally resilient parent accepts that the ironing and other chores need to be done and just gets on with it).

Managing Emotions

The way feelings are handled or managed is crucial to developing emotional literacy. People who are good at managing emotions don't have any less powerful emotions, but they do routinely take responsibility for their feelings and (as above) commit to action in trying to handle overwhelming feelings more effectively. Effective management of emotions implies a prerequisite average or better self-awareness, and resolution to use feelings positively. Being able to manage emotions well confers advantage in many settings, but particularly improves emotional resilience to major life events such as moving home, changing jobs, redundancy, marital breakdown, or bereavement. People who are good at managing emotions are better able to express emotions, and do so in a way that is timely and doesn't violate the best interests of others. Higgs and Dulewicz incorporate another element under this heading which they call 'Conscientiousness and Integrity', which encompasses the individual's ability to accept personal responsibility and accountability for their actions and decisions as well as being open and transparent in their dealings with others.

Managing emotions: a worked example

A teacher is told that a colleague who is leaving won't be replaced because of budget problems, and the new timetable means that she will lose non-contact time and be expected to teach two extra groups from September. The teacher recognises that the budget problem is real and acknowledges that some sacrifice may be needed. She chooses a time to discuss the matter calmly with the Deputy Head and explains her feelings that having no non-contact time means all her classes may suffer as she's already substantially over-working in order to prepare lessons well and keep up with her formative assessments. Even if there is no change in the eventual outcome, the teacher is at least pleased that she was heard and that her concerns centred on her ability to do her job well, and she may even acknowledge that redundancies have been avoided by this plan.

Motivating oneself

Harnessing or using emotions to achieve a goal is a core skill for developing emotional literacy. In Freudian terms the *superego* holds the *id* in check by reducing impulsivity and keeping the goal as paramount. People with high self-motivation are able to focus and concentrate well, and to channel both their cognitive and affective skills into achievement-oriented behaviour. A highly emotionally literate person is able to do this while still taking full account of the feelings of others. People with low self-motivation are inclined to be overwhelmed by affective states, sometimes to the point of paralysis, and so rarely 'get the job done'. Goleman (1996) says that accomplishment of every sort is based on emotional self-control, whereby gratification is delayed and impulsiveness stifled.

Motivating oneself: a worked example

A very busy and successful class teacher, who also enjoys spending time with her family, decides to study for a higher degree so as to prepare herself for later headship. By necessity the course has to be part-time, and in order to stay on top of her other commitments, she enrols at the Open University and works regularly in the late evenings, weekends, and at summer school. Despite all the competing demands she completes her Master's degree on time in just two years.

Empathy

Showing fellow feeling or empathy is the basis of all interpersonal skills. An ability to read and tune in to other people's feelings is a core skill in letting people feel acknowledged and valued. It involves seeing the world through other people's eyes, even or especially when their unenviable predicament is of their own making. At a more subtle and sophisticated level it means responding appropriately to other people's moods, temperaments and motivations. Demonstrating empathy may require the subjugation of personal moods or affective states, if the person being attended to has a greater need. People in the caring professions usually show a high degree of empathy, but it is a core skill in all work involving people.

Empathy: a worked example

You've just got a promotion at work, which means recognition of your talent and a bit more money, but then you meet a friend at a pub who looks miserable. Rather than blurt out your good news and overwhelm your friend you ask how she's feeling, thereby giving her the chance to say why she's looking so fed up. It transpires that she's just had a miscarriage, so you buy her a drink and invite her to talk about it if that's what she wants to do. After going through the whole story and offering an attentive listening ear your friend then says she has to get home, but thanks you for being so understanding. Somehow it just didn't feel appropriate to raise the subject of your good news, even though it was still fresh and exciting for you, but you found a better moment when you called a few days later and first checked how she was feeling.

Handling Relationships

This skill incorporates all of the above, but more besides. In recognising that conflict is a part of everyday life, it also covers our ability to manage that conflict in an emotionally literate way. For Steiner (1997) it includes knowing how and when to apologise and make amends for mistakes. For Goleman it includes all the abilities that go to make up popularity, leadership, and interpersonal effectiveness. Within the work context, Higgs and Dulewicz (1999) describe it as: 'the ability to manage relationships in order to achieve results,' and thus it entails the ability to persuade others to work as individuals and in teams to achieve important work-related goals. Steiner concludes with a higher order category called 'emotional interactivity' whereby you connect more fully with others around you.

Higgs and Dulewicz have added other skills or competencies to this broader category. The first is 'Making Decisions in Complex Interpersonal Situations', which requires an ability to cope with stress (particularly that arising from emotional conflict) and to maintain and deliver performance when under pressure.

Handling relationships: a worked example

A head teacher is appointed to a primary school, having been the infant school head, following the amalgamation of her infant school with the neighbouring junior school. The junior school staff like their current head and had hoped she would be appointed; instead she is to take very early retirement. The infant head handles the situation with tact and care by approaching her soon-to-retire colleague and tells her she knows that it must be extremely tough to be giving up the school she's done so much for, but asks for her advice on how to get the best start in September for all the staff and children of the new school. The two heads are able to form a working partnership, albeit a bit strained, because they're both able to focus on getting it right for the children and all the staff. They both display a high level of emotional literacy, and the integrity of the junior school head is beyond reproach.

Taking care of yourself

Now that we've started to unpack the competencies of emotional literacy, let's move on to building emotional literacy. The first step in taking care of yourself is to believe you have the right to! Many of us are now so busy taking care of others, or of business, that we forget to look after ourselves.

Self-help can only work if you commit to an action plan and then do your best to hold to it. This will involve building on the 'taking stock' activities described in Chapter 2, and then identifying personal goals. Someone once said 'a goal without a date is but a dream', so dream first and then set a date!

In essence, taking care of yourself involves developing a passion for the positive, so that negative thoughts and mind sets are avoided or, better still, banished. Getting your own needs met sometimes means a temporary subjugation for the feelings and needs of other adults. Let's assume that we can honour our basic and essential responsibilities to others, especially children, then we can best help them further by helping ourselves to become emotionally and physically healthy. Accessible and useful 'pop psychology' books that can help you to achieve this include *She Who Dares Wins* by Eileen Gillibrand and Jenny Mosley, as well as *Super Confidence* by Gail Lindenfield. Gillibrand and Mosley (1995) assert that their book is written by and for women, but the excellent and sound advice that appears is hardly gender specific, but rather about taking care of yourself, being positive and setting out a written contract with yourself.

Taking care of yourself incorporates meeting basic needs (physiological and safety needs), a degree of pampering, and social needs. However, if you want to move towards self-actualisation then it also involves some challenge. Set out below are some ideas to begin nurturing our own emotional literacy:

> To be true to ourselves a career should be planned within the context of our vocation or calling. In no way does this limit us. Choosing to focus our talents toward what we truly love and believe in brings forth the creativity, energy, and commitment that are key characteristics of any successful career. You will discover that your career goals are much more readily achieved when you are working on purpose.
> (McNally 1993)

Allow yourself to be yourself

So nurturing *your* emotional literacy involves recognition of who you are and choosing what you do, and for some people this may be very challenging and require significant change to their lifestyle. There are many people that 'fall into' particular jobs, but if you want to nurture your own emotional literacy then recognise that only you have the responsibility to change what you don't like, or otherwise learn to live with who you are and what you do. Emotional literacy may be nurtured whether you have a 'career' or not, but however your waking hours are spent will be determined by how emotionally literate you are.

Allowing yourself to be yourself involves the acceptance of a paradox, namely that '...we feel better when we attempt to make our world better... to have a purpose beyond one's self lends to existence a meaning and direction – the most important characteristic of high well-being. (Sheehy 1993). So the contribution we make to others may have little to do with visible rewards, and more to do with what is in our hearts, made real by choosing how and when to help or care for others.

A further conundrum is posed by consideration of the need to like or love yourself as you are, while being prepared to change or adapt parts of yourself that are blocking development.

David Whyte, poet and author, said: '98.98 per cent of everything that you do or say is for your self and... there isn't one.' Only you can know your 'self', because others only know a part of you.

Most people find it hard to recognise and prize their strengths, and are only too aware of their weaknesses and limitations. Nurturing your own emotional literacy involves concentrating and building on your strengths.

Hansen and Batten (1995) describe a process for achieving this development using a *'blueprint for one-on-one motivation'*, shown in Figure 3.1.

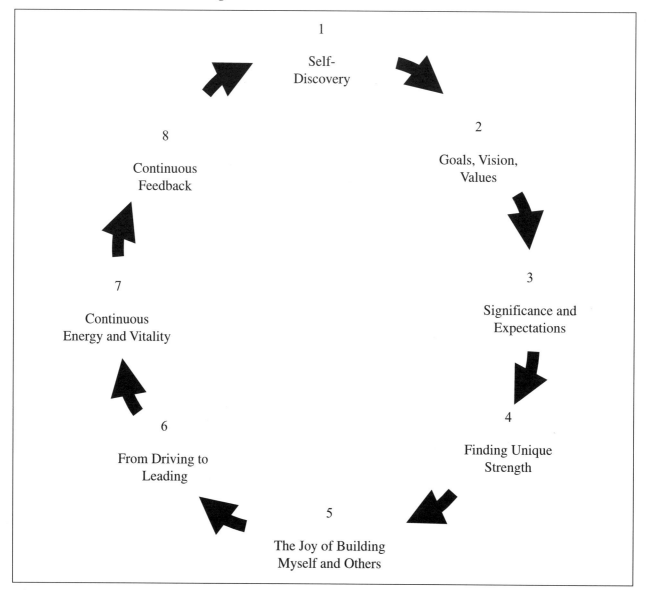

Figure 3.1   Concentrating and building on your strengths

In essence then, taking care of yourself is a continuous cycle, or virtuous circle, whereby we make time to reflect, review, and implement any actions that we feel are needed.

Each of us needs a purpose and our own answer to the universally challenging question: 'Why are we here?' Our answer may be a combination of the rational and the affective, or it may incline more in just one direction. For some a leap of faith leads down a spiritual path, for others it may be a simple reductionist biological perspective, and for yet others there may be a complex and even dynamic answer. William James distinguished between the self-as-subject or knower ('I') and the self-as-known or object ('me'). The 'I' is the main form of the self and at the centre of our consciousness, but the self is multi-faceted and we change our behaviour depending on many factors including whom we are with.

Our self-concept is made up of our self-image (how we perceive our self), self-esteem (how we regard our self), and our ideal-self (how we would like to see our self, sometimes called the ego-ideal). The notion of the 'looking-glass self' implies that we need to see how others see us, and this in turn leads to us seeing how we are evaluated or judged. Denzin (1995) extrapolated this view to say that the individual and society are opposite sides of the same coin, though this contrasts with the work of George Herbert Mead who asserted that the self is not mentalistic or private but rather a cognitive process rooted in the social world.

In order to understand ourselves and to make sense of our experiences we engage in discourses, and these are culture bound, so that self-concept is culture bound too. The poet David Whyte says:

> No-one has to change but we must have the conversation, and when we get all of the conversations out of the way then we'll just do it.

He related this comment to a central theme that emotional intelligence is:

> ...a territory that lies ahead of us, and every human being belongs to their own horizon... and our best endeavour is to walk to that (our) horizon.

In effect then, we all need to develop a vision of who we are and who we want to be, and this will be underpinned by a set of personal values. In nurturing our own emotional literacy we can establish personal goals, and then work towards them. In practical terms this can be achieved by simply writing down our vision, listing our values, then specifying short-, medium-, and long-term goals. Sharing these thoughts with trusted significant others may also support us in making them happen, and may help us recognise that life is dynamic and the review process is iterative and subject to events beyond our personal control. It is also true that we have more chance of enhancing our own emotional literacy if we are fostering the development of other people's emotional literacy, whether they are our partners, children, friends, relatives, colleagues or professional responsibilities.

Reflect on your vision, values and goals

Enhance your self-esteem

If I had my child to raise all over again, I'd finger paint more, and point the finger less.
I'd do less correcting, and more connecting.
I'd take my eyes off my watch, and watch with my eyes.
I would care to know less, and know to care more.
I'd take more hikes and fly more kites.
I'd stop playing serious, and seriously play.
I would run through more fields and gaze at more stars.
I'd do more hugging and less tugging.
I would be firm less often, and affirm much more.
I'd build self-esteem first, and the house later.
I'd teach less about the love of power, and more about the power of love.
Diane Loomans
'Full Esteem Ahead'

How we regard our self is fundamental to how we regard and treat others, so that while self-image is a description of how we see our self, the evaluation of that image or perception is our self-esteem. Coopersmith (1967) defines self-esteem as: 'a personal judgement of worthiness that is expressed in the attitudes the individual holds towards himself.' Clearly then, an emotionally literate person will have high self-esteem that is validated and endorsed by significant others. Our self-esteem is also determined in part by the gap between our self-image and our ideal-self (the person we would like to be). So self-esteem can be promoted, developed and nurtured through a number of routes including:

- developing accurate self-image – based on reality checks, understanding the relative nature of comparison, and accurate feedback from trusted significant others;
- attaining ideal-self – based on real possibilities and not perfectionism;
- fostering unconditional positive self-regard, and aiming to see the positive in others too;
- achieving goals, and setting achievable but challenging standards;
- creating opportunities to succeed and celebrating even partial success;
- avoiding negative thinking and negative thinkers;
- seeking daily affirmation through marking or noting steps to success.

Each of us has a set of personal and family scripts; some of which are empowering and a boost to promoting self-esteem, while others simply hold us back, or worse, reduce our self-esteem. An example of a positive personal script is when we believe that we are loveable because our parents regularly told us and showed us that we are, or simply because they did openly love us. This in turn is likely to make us more secure, better able to take some risks in relationships, to think well of others, and to expect to succeed generally. Contrast that with a negative script arrived at as a consequence of endless parental put-downs, unfavourable comparisons with siblings or other children and a generally punitive or hostile parental experience.

Unsurprisingly, people with negative scripts have low self-esteem because the gap between their poor self-image and their ideal-self is so wide.

In order to enhance your self-esteem begin by aiming to have positive self-belief, focus on any previous success and savour any affirmation or praise you received and believe in your value as someone with skills, talents, abilities and aptitudes. So begins a virtuous circle that leads to a more positive self-image; and self-confidence is projected to others, who will see you as capable and having much to offer. The next segment of the circle will lead to high expectations both of yourself and from others, so that a self-fulfilling prophecy will in turn result in more opportunities for success and ultimately enhanced performance. Gillibrand and Mosley (1995) describe the above as 'the upward spiral of sound self-esteem' and also describe 'the downward spiral of low self-esteem'. Suffice to say that we all need to take charge of our own belief systems, whatever the historical antecedents to our current levels of self-esteem, and to aim for a positive mind set that fosters a belief in our capacity to succeed and to develop.

If, while reading this, you feel it is persecutory or wildly unrealistic then the chances are that you have had numerous very tough experiences and you may need some support to move on, either from trusted friends or a professional counsellor or psychologist. If the prospect of that is daunting then go for self-help and get the book *She Who Dares Wins*.

It is important to recognise that self-esteem is not static, but rather is dynamic, and no one is immune from either negative events or negative influences (e.g. some people, aspects of the media). The important issue in enhancing your self-esteem, as one component of your emotional literacy, is to take responsibility for how you react to negative events such as redundancy, marital break-up, accidents, or illness. Gillibrand and Mosley give ten ways to challenge negative thinking:

1. Be realistic – reframe negative thoughts and discard distorted thinking.
2. Search for the truth – rethink and express beliefs or thoughts accurately.
3. Examine the pros and cons – evaluate the benefit/harm a thought is having on your life.
4. Be kind to yourself – forgive yourself as you would others.
5. Face up to your fears – resolve to work on the fears positively.
6. Banish generalisations – specific negative behaviour may not be generalised.
7. Focus on all the factors – hold on to perspective and proportion by considering all relevant information.
8. Check or clarify your perceptions – Assumptions can be false.
9. Check the validity of your feelings – it may be that you're entitled to feel negative but think how best to handle those feelings.
10. Accept your negative thoughts – all feelings are normal, and it's good to recognise the difficulties some create for you.

Enhancing self-esteem can be a slow process, especially if you had few deposits in your emotional bank account when younger, but start now and you'll see benefits right away and so will other people in your circle. If self-awareness is the foundation of emotional literacy then enhancing self-esteem lies at the heart of the nurturing process.

Take charge of your thoughts and choose your attitude

An attitude is a relatively enduring orientation that we hold towards objects, issues, events, places, and people, it is generally expressed publicly as opinion, and it is notoriously difficult to change. Fontana (1995) notes that: 'Attitudes clearly contain elements of value and belief, as well as varying degrees of factual knowledge (or what the holder takes to be factual knowledge), and possess cognitive and behavioural as well as affective aspects.' The interaction between the cognitive and affective aspects of attitudes needs to be further explored if we are to nurture our own emotional literacy. Some attitudes are openly expressed and are wholly conscious, while others are kept repressed in the unconscious but find expression in unpleasant and/or surreptitious acts. For example, an extrovert may consciously express the attitude that they like people who are as outgoing as they are (a conscious reaction), but in another extrovert the same attitude may be repressed and be expressed through a surreptitious act, say of recruiting only extroverts to their team, or blocking promotion of introverts. Freudian thinkers hold the conflict between conscious and unconscious attitudes to be pivotal in the development of the personality, but given that we are considering how to take charge of our thoughts and choose our attitude then we'll need to focus on conscious attitudes. If, however, you are keen to develop this further, then it is possible to work on making the unconscious conscious through therapy, analysis, or dream-work with a qualified psychologist, psychotherapist or analyst.

Whatever your age, the essence of who you are has been enmeshed in beliefs and assumptions about yourself and others. From early childhood these began accumulating and have led to your current attitudes. Many of your conclusions, some assumptions, and even some beliefs are faulty as they are based on erroneous information. They are true for you only because you believe them to be so. The next task is to list limiting thoughts and beliefs and try to reframe them, for example: 'I'm stuck in this job and there is no way out or forward and I don't enjoy my work any more.' This could be reframed into 'I need to review why I'm doing the job I do and try to identify which bits of it I like and which I dislike'. If the reframe causes too much cognitive or affective dissonance – it's just too provoking – then maybe you do need thoroughly to review where you'd like to be working and then plan how to get there.

Stephen Covey (1999) describes a habit as the intersection of knowledge, skill, and desire. He adds: 'Knowledge is the theoretical paradigm, the *what to do* and the *why*. Skill is the *how to do*. And desire is the motivation, the *want to do*.' To have a positive attitude and to develop emotional literacy requires all three, and is the basis of becoming proactive and so more effective. Covey goes on to describe how being proactive, beginning with the end in mind and putting first things first, are all private victories and need to be achieved before moving on to public victories. Essentially, having the right attitude increases the likelihood of achieving your goals within an ethical context whereby you don't violate the best interests of others.

Very few people have a real sense of what they want from life, much less a determination to go and get it, or perhaps more significantly to 'be it'. Having a positive attitude is a personal choice, sometimes a triumph over adversity, and there are many seductive cynics who would like to lure you into their gloom. A more emotionally literate person, however, recognises that the process of looking for the positive is often difficult and exhausting, but is not overwhelmed by that prospect for too long. To change our attitudes often requires a major shift in a personal or family script and it therefore involves a change in the inner dialogue. Achieving this requires a high degree of self-awareness and listening to an inner voice, rather than projecting the blame out onto others for how we end up feeling. This is not to say that other people are not responsible in any way for our feelings, but rather that we are ultimately responsible for what we do with those feelings.

Essentially we are all prone to being swamped by problems, negative forces and feelings, and our challenge is to shake off the negative and look for the positive... to turn problems into opportunities.

Problems or opportunities?

A life without problems is a fantasy, and many people have personal problems of such a magnitude that they drown in them, or end their own lives. The business or motivational speaker's cliché: 'there are no such things as problems only opportunities' is experienced by many as persecutory and trite. Therapists who assert that their clients should move straight to solutions are negating often long and tortuous struggles endured by their clients. People sometimes *need* to wrestle with and even wallow in problems before becoming unstuck enough to find their own appropriate solutions. What is useful though, is to develop the mind set that says problems can be turned into opportunities, or that some opportunities arise only because there was a problem.

John Kehoe (1997) describes how problems and difficulties can be used as a springboard to deeper insight, and gives the example of researcher Don Stookey who accidentally left some treated glass in a furnace for so long that it turned white. Undaunted, Stookey creatively turned that accident into a benefit by continuing to experiment with the new substance and, when he found it could withstand searing heat, further refined and marketed his mistake as Corning Ware. At a more personal level Kehoe also describes how Gail Devers was training to compete at the 1992 Barcelona Olympics when she broke out in sores all over her body, later diagnosed as Graves' disease. Doctors told her she would have to have her feet amputated, but two days before the operation she began improving. She later went on to win the 100 metre race in Barcelona and repeated the feat in Atlanta in 1996. Gail said: 'I wouldn't change a thing, it was a blessing. It made me a stronger, better person.'

So adversity, or problems, can be turned inside out. Jeff Keller (1999) describes how adversity can serve us on seven levels:

1. Adversity gives us perspective: and we all know how life-threatening events or bereavement can help us to regain a sense of what is really important.
2. Adversity teaches us to be grateful for the many blessings we normally take for granted: and while we may lose the immediate appreciation of what we have got with the passage of time, most people can continue to recognise their good fortune long after facing a loss or difficulty.
3. Adversity strengthens us and allows us to discover a reservoir of previously untapped abilities: when we solve a problem or simply survive a difficulty then we emerge stronger, especially if we struggled and rose to a challenge.
4. Adversity encourages us to make changes and take action: interestingly the older we get the more traumatic or provoking an event needs to be in order to bring about enduring or significant change.
5. From adversity, we gain valuable knowledge which we can use at a later date: so if we have a relationship break-up then later we may be able to make use of the lessons learned and avoid the same mistakes or behaviour patterns.
6. A problem or difficulty leads us to something better: when people are made redundant or the business folds it seems like the world has collapsed, but it could represent the chance to begin again and even in a better job.
7. Overcoming adversity makes you feel better about yourself: at some time we all have self-doubt or a crisis in confidence, for some this is potentially devastating, but for others conquering a fear, an illness, a tragic loss is at the heart of personal growth.

The more emotionally literate we become, the more likely we are to recognise the potential for turning problems into opportunities. Having established the importance of attitude and the need for positive thinking let's go on to look at how optimism can be learned, even by people who see the hole and not the doughnut!

The pessimist looks at these glasses and sees them as half-empty, while the optimist is pleased to see them as half-full and is just pleased to have a drink!

Is your glass half-empty or half-full?

Glass Half-Empty   Glass Half-Full

Optimistic people who suffer setbacks tend to attribute them to external causes that are temporary and can be changed. Pessimistic people believe that the setbacks are inevitable, and caused by internal causes that are permanent and not amenable to change. Professor Andrew Steptoe, of St George's Hospital Medical School, says that a psychological analysis of Mozart's correspondence shows that he was almost pathologically optimistic, with an exuberant self-confidence. Towards the end of Mozart's short life, when he suffered the deaths of four children, serious illnesses and repeated professional and financial disasters, his optimism actually rose.

Martin Seligman, director of training at the University of Pennsylvania in Philadelphia, has developed an Attributional Style Questionnaire (ASQ), which ranks individuals on an optimism-pessimism scale. In a longitudinal study of school children, those scoring highest for pessimism were most likely later to suffer depression. High scores for optimism are predictive of excellence in everything from sports to life-insurance sales. Seligman describes how optimists, even when offered a monetary incentive for accuracy, consistently overestimate their ability. He asserts that optimists have a set of self-serving illusions that enable them to maintain good cheer and health in a universe essentially indifferent to their welfare. Seligman goes further by saying that optimists are more resistant to infectious illness and are better at fending off chronic diseases of middle age. In one study of 96 men who had a heart attack in 1980, 15 out of 16 of the most pessimistic died of a second heart attack, whereas only 6 out of 16 of the most optimistic men had died.

Seligman believes that optimism can be learned, and that learned optimism may entail bolstering a set of benign illusions. He argues that depressed people may need to adopt the same self-serving illusions that most normal people hold, and advises that pessimists should speak to themselves more kindly, the way a loving friend might. A pessimist may say: 'I'll never get it right', or 'I always mess up'. Instead, it could help to learn to say: 'OK, things didn't go well today, but I learned a lot from the experience, and I'll do better tomorrow.' Similarly, instead of negative labels such as 'I'm useless at caring', positively reframe into 'Sometimes I'm not as considerate as I'd like to be, but overall I'm a kind person'. To overcome pessimism Seligman further advises that we should not ruminate about bad events that happen to us, at least not immediately afterwards. Instead look for pleasurable distractions from your troubles, because studies show that thinking about problems in a negative frame of mind generates fewer solutions, and can result in a downward spiral into deeper depression. Boosting mood and self-esteem can break the negative cycle and free people to think more creatively.

There are strong links between optimism, thinking, and creativity. Pessimists may be right, in terms of accuracy, more often than optimists are, but optimists accomplish more. Edward de Bono (1967) has shown that even in the face of a rigorous proof that there is no solution, a different way of defining the original problem can lead to a solution. Often we believe there is no solution but there is a fallacy somewhere in the argument we've used to convince ourselves of this. Creative thinking can jump across those barriers. Given below are some suggestions based on de Bono's creativity techniques that can help with problem-solving and enhancing optimism:

1. Stop thinking about the problem for a time: come back to it fresh and do something different and unrelated in the meantime.
2. Think of analogous problems: come up with the way you solved those problems and see if any of the techniques can be used to solve this new problem.
3. Write down the problem: then translate it into different languages or from words into images (drawings, photo-montage, clipart) so that different vocabularies or styles of thought can be provoked or invoked, and may give insight into tackling a seemingly insurmountable difficulty.
4. Explain the problem to someone else: oddly enough, telling someone who knows nothing about the problem can give a fresh take on how you might see the problem, or at least help you to explain it differently.
5. Sleep on it: there is persuasive evidence that solutions or part-solutions occur to us when we stop looking for them!
6. Dream on it: think about it just before you go to sleep, and have paper and pen or a tape-recorder by your bed, because you may

wake up with what seems wacky but helps you solve the problem.

7. Put up photos, images, rich pictures, words, or phrases: around your home or workplace that may trigger thoughts at odd moments.

8. Begin with the end in mind, imagine what a solution might look like: then you can work backwards.

Many of the techniques above have been used to help find solutions to technical or academic problems, but most people spend far more time worrying about 'people problems' or relationships than technical problems. So the more emotionally literate we become the more sophisticated and creative we may become in managing our emotions.

In this chapter we have covered both *why* and *how* to nurture our emotional literacy, including some very practical steps to follow. As you read this you may have picked up a few ideas and be planning to implement them or to simply mull them over with other people, but a real commitment to action involves you in making a contract with yourself to do something more. Your commitment to action would be even more likely to happen if you shared your plan with a trusted and valued colleague, friend or partner.

Commit to action

Summary of Chapter 3: Nurturing your Emotional Literacy

Skills and competencies of Emotional Literacy include:

- Self-awareness
- Managing emotions
- Motivation
- Empathy
- Handling Relationships.

Take care of yourself by developing a passion for the positive, and learn to like yourself more as you are.

Allow yourself to be yourself by building on your strengths, and affirming your right to be well regarded.

Reflect on your vision, values and goals by daring to dream, then building a vision, then set some goals and set a date to achieve them.

Enhance your self-esteem by narrowing the gap between your self-image and your ideal-self.

Choose your attitude because your attitude determines your altitude, and you *do* have choice.

No problems, only opportunities or at least that could be your ambition to *see* problems as potential opportunities.

Is your glass half-empty or half-full? Learn to be even more optimistic and you'll live better and maybe even longer.

Make a contract with yourself and share it: Personal Action Plan

Nurturing your Emotional Literacy: Commit to action

List one action for promoting each of the following skills or competencies:

- Self-awareness:

- Managing emotions:

- Motivation:

- Empathy:

- Handling relationships:

What I like about myself:

-

-

-

-

-

The strengths I want to build on are:

-

-

-

-

-

My vision:

My values:

My goals:

How I will promote my self-esteem:

How I will become even more optimistic:

An example of how I turned a problem into an opportunity:

Name _____ Date _____

Who I will share this with _____

Chapter 4

Emotional Literacy for teachers and learners

Our chief want in life is somebody who will make us do what we can.
Ralph Waldo Emerson

So far this book has centred on personal development, almost irrespective of role or job or vocation. This chapter is aimed squarely at teachers and learners and sets out to describe how we may nurture a more emotionally literate educative process mediated by more emotionally literate teachers, hopefully in the context of a more emotionally literate society.

Emotional literacy of teachers and learners

Teachers and learners, and teachers as learners, can only thrive and learn well if the national climate fosters their development. A more emotionally literate society will only become a reality if government and other influential decision makers make a conscious and determined effort to reward and regard teachers and educators more highly. It simply isn't good enough to have ever-higher expectations of teachers and educators while using the poor psychology of naming and shaming the under-performers as the central strategy for driving up standards. As well as additional targeted resources, we need a climate that fosters development and allows teachers and educators to nurture emotional literacy without the unnecessary fear induced by a punitive and shortsighted quality assurance system that over-focuses on attainment measures.

The Teacher Support Network established a telephone helpline for teachers in 1999 and during the first year of operating 'Teacherline' (0800 562 561), there were over 12,000 calls seeking advice, support or guidance. Of the 12,000 callers 27 per cent had high levels of stress, anxiety or depression, and a significant number had already visited their doctor before calling. This confirms a widely held view that teachers are finding it increasingly hard to balance their lives and meet the challenges faced in trying to promote school effectiveness, raise standards, and yet make the educative process holistic, enjoyable, and sustainable. Paradoxically, the emotional literacy of teachers may be falling because they are often concentrating first on meeting the needs of learners. In a recent survey of 2,700 young people in Brighton and Hove it was found that 20 per cent have serious behavioural and emotional problems (*TES* 27 October 2000), which suggest that it is not just the teachers that have high levels of mental health difficulties.

The difficulties facing both teachers and learners are beginning to be recognised and government departments have started to address them. The Healthy Schools Initiative, involving both the Department of Health and the Department for Education and Employment, has elaborated strategies for improving teacher health and well-being:

1. Developing health awareness programmes for staff;
2. Appropriate management of recurrent sickness absence;
3. Ensuring highest standards of physical safety for the whole school community;
4. Identification of sources of stress and managing it;
5. Promoting physical activity for staff;
6. Support systems (for all);
7. Enhanced support systems (for some individuals);
8. Making appraisal systems useful for staff and the school;
9. Management of time and rationalisation of administration;
10. Encouraging communication with the whole school community.

More details of this can be found at the website: *www.dfee.gov.uk/hsht/contents.htm*

In addition, the pressing emotional or mental health needs of young people have also begun to be addressed by government, as evidenced by the establishment of a website for teenagers located at: *www.mindbodysoul.gov.uk*

The website includes reference to accidents, alcohol, drugs, healthy eating, mental health, physical activity, sexual health, smoking, and sun safety. The section on mental health includes:

- take time for yourself
- let out your emotions
- see friends
- talk about it.

Each of these sections has advice and guidance, for example the information on 'Let out your emotions' describes how anger management can help young people.

So there is at least recognition at governmental level that the emotional needs of both teachers and learners must be attended to. However, this chapter is aimed at what teachers can do to promote their own emotional literacy and in turn the emotional literacy of learners.

Professor Tim Brighouse (2000) refers to some of the qualities of a good teacher or head teacher as 'constant characteristics', and these include:

- being infectiously optimistic
- being a good listener
- showing commitment
- being a taker of blame and a celebrator of others
- having a clear philosophy.

If a significant number of staff in a school were to have these qualities then the emotional climate and the school culture would be electric, and the resultant impact on the organisational emotional literacy would be reflected in the improving emotional literacy of the teachers and the learners. Per Dalin (1995) said that: 'The only way schools will survive the future is to become creative learning organizations. The best way students can learn how to live in the future is to experience the life of the 'learning school'.'

In a study by Steven Stein and Howard Book (2000) of 4,888 people in a mixed population, the five most important factors linked to overall success were:

1. Self-actualisation
2. Happiness
3. Optimism
4. Self-regard
5. Assertiveness.

By contrast, the factors found to be of greatest significance for teachers were:

Secondary School Teachers – 200 teachers	**Primary School Teachers** – 347 teachers
1. Empathy	1. Optimism
2. Self-actualisation	2. Self-regard
3. Stress Tolerance.	3. Independence
	4. Stress Tolerance
	5. Happiness.

A related group classified by Stein and Book as 'Education Workers' had other factors listed as the most significant for this population (168 people):

1. Interpersonal Relationships
2. Reality Testing
3. Optimism
4. Happiness
5. Self-regard.

It is interesting to note then that even variations in the age group taught or the specific job in education may require quite different strengths in teachers and others involved in the educative process.

Research into teacher effectiveness carried out by Hay McBer (2000) found three main factors within teachers' control that significantly influence pupil progress:

- Teaching skills
- Professional characteristics
- Classroom climate.

The report describes the professional characteristics as 'the ongoing patterns of behaviour that combine to drive the things we typically do' and the teaching skills as the 'micro-behaviours' that can be learned.

Hay McBer grouped teaching skills under the seven OFSTED inspection headings: high expectations, planning, methods and strategies, pupil management and discipline, time and resource management, assessment, and homework. The professional characteristics were described under five clusters: professionalism, thinking, planning and setting expectations, leading, and relating to others. I would argue that emotional literacy is a combination of knowledge, skills, experience and feelings and that personal characteristics underpin *all* professional characteristics. The Hay McBer research is useful in pointing out that teaching skills can be learned, but misses the opportunity to make it explicit that emotional literacy can also be learned and developed. If emotional literacy is fostered then so too will 'professional characteristics' be improved.

Hay McBer defines classroom climate as the collective perceptions by pupils of what it feels like to be a pupil in any particular teacher's classroom. A positive classroom climate includes 'feeling emotionally supported in the classroom, so that pupils are willing to try new things and learn from mistakes'. The creation of a positive classroom (and school) climate is only really possible when both the teacher and the learners, and the teacher as a learner, are actively engaged in promoting emotional literacy. As one Year 7 pupil told me in an anger management group: 'the teacher's job is to civilise the classroom.'

Teachers can only help learners to improve their emotional literacy significantly if they have first addressed their own needs. Emotional literacy is not static or linear, but dynamic and multi-faceted, and emotional literacy needs to be included in 'professional characteristics' and seen as essential to good teaching.

Emotional literacy and the curriculum

The 'hidden curriculum' is all that occurs in a school beyond the explicit 'taught curriculum'. Taken together the whole curriculum will determine how emotionally literate a school is and the individuals within it. Our definition of emotional literacy as 'the ability to recognise, understand, handle, and appropriately express emotions', is incremental and based on first having an extensive feelings vocabulary. This then leads on to developing some understanding of those feelings both cognitively and affectively, and later to being better able to handle feelings effectively. At a much later stage, and a higher order competence, is the ability to express feelings appropriately, taking account of a range of factors including: context, importance, safety, security, humanity and desirability. So emotional literacy can be 'taught' and 'caught', and children will begin school with embedded emotional competence or incompetence.

The emotional literacy taught and caught curriculum in a school will include:

- *Conscious awareness*, particularly as evidenced by the development of an extensively expressed feelings vocabulary.
- *Understanding thoughts*, feelings and actions as they relate to learning and achievement, decision-making and relationships.
- *Managing feelings* so that we can be more effective in meeting our needs without violating the interests of others.
- *Promoting self-esteem* so that people feel good about themselves and about each other.
- *Managing conflict* to achieve better-for-both outcomes through effective anger management and better interpersonal skills.
- *Understanding groups* so that we can contribute more effectively in group settings.
- *Communication skills* to promote appropriate expression of feelings and thoughts, which implies the ability to give and receive love.

There is a place for an explicit taught curriculum with explicit schemes of work, lesson plans, and using a range of teaching methods and accommodating different learning styles, and there is also a need to 'live the emotional literacy curriculum' in schools. In order to devise policies, procedures, and practices that nurture emotional literacy, schools can carry out a curriculum audit to see where they are, and to inform the plan of where they want to be. Firstly they need to gather together all their documentation relating to the areas given in Table 4.1 below.

Emotional Literacy encompasses:

> Learning and achievement	> Equal Opportunities
> Health Promotion	> Citizenship
> Personal, Social and Health Education	> Behaviour and Discipline
	> Social Inclusion
> Spiritual, Moral, Social and Cultural Development	> Crime and Disorder

---

Table 4.1 The human aspects of curriculum – what emotional literacy encompasses

Having gathered all the documentation they have on the areas listed above, and few schools will have policies on them all, then the whole staff needs to be engaged in a detailed and far-reaching debate about the compatibility of all these statements. Experience suggests that this is best done in the school hall with long tables and multiple copies of the documentation, each with 'header cards' labelling the title, nature and status of the documents, (e.g. Policy draft, working group report, notes, work in progress, etc.). The key features of each area need to listed and examined before exploring compatibility and consistency issues. For example, most equal opportunities policies or statements begin with a statement like: 'We value and respect everyone, irrespective of race, colour, creed, gender, and …', whereas the behaviour and discipline policy may begin in exactly the same way but then move on to say what happens in the event that a pupil does not conform to a long and often complex set of rules and expectations. This is not to say that there is anything inherently wrong with the incompatibility, merely to point up the inherent tension of there being two very different policies. Few, if any schools, have compiled *all* their policies with regard to consistency, compatibility and constancy. In an emotionally literate school such matters will be regarded as important and attempts will be made to address these issues so that both the taught and the caught curriculum are well considered and explicitly described.

An example of a taught emotional literacy curriculum is afforded by the imaginative and valuable work done by Sue Nicholson (head teacher) and the staff at Mason Moor Primary School in Southampton. Following a school closure used to introduce emotional literacy to all the staff (teachers, learning support assistants, office staff, governors), an extensive programme of activities was undertaken. These included benchmarking all the pupils' emotional literacy skills using a checklist, establishing a baseline for current levels of behaviour and misbehaviour, then devising a scheme of work for every child and member of staff to be engaged in and all this to be incorporated in the revised school development plan. The school devised a draft two-year cycle Emotional Literacy scheme of work for Year R (Reception Class) to Year 6 and incorporated a rigorous evaluation and monitoring system.

The Mason Moor Primary School draft scheme of work included:

- adopt key feeling(s) each half term (i.e. 12 feelings per year);
- contrast any negative feeling with a positive;
- first session to benchmark existing 'feelings' vocabulary;
- further sessions using drama, role play, etc;
- explore body language;
- use Circle Time;
- assembly themes;
- fiction/library links;
- central theme displays;
- music/colour imagery;
- all adults to model, extend, rehearse new 'feelings' vocabulary;
- evaluation at end.

Each class worked on a range of feelings, usually bipolar or contrasting and explored through a variety of teaching methods. For example:

Term	Year 1	Year 2
Autumn 1	angry/calm	lonely/sociable
Autumn 2	surprised (good/bad)	greedy/generous
Spring 1	bored/interested	jealous/content
Spring 2	sad/happy	loving
Summer 1	intimidated/confident	afraid/brave
Summer 2	ashamed/proud	enjoyment

Table 4.2   Mason Moor Primary School – Draft Scheme of work for Y1 and Y2 Feelings

The resources used to support this work included games, simulations, puppets, pictures, photographs, displays around the school, books and other media. This work is currently being formally evaluated, and there is sufficient qualitative evidence to ensure continued support from staff, parents and governors. Convincing quantitative evidence of change is unlikely to be found after just one year of implementation, though the green shoots of change are being seen. There is also a recognition that this kind of work may not feed through to impacting on embedded attitudes for some time, and will also vary in its effectiveness with each individual child or teacher. Even so, the value of having a taught curriculum for emotional literacy can be measured if many more schools engage in this kind of work, and then share their experience and pool data. At Mason Moor Primary there is a clear link to raising achievement for all pupils along with promoting emotional literacy.

Emotional literacy guidelines

Southampton Emotional Literacy Interest Group (SELIG) was established in 1999 by Southampton Education Services, and has a membership of 21 people comprising:

Principal Educational Psychologist (Chair)	Head teachers
Chief Inspector (Vice Chair)	Teachers
Principal Secondary Inspector	Teacher Advisers
University representative	Education officers
Consultant Psychiatrist	Governor
Social Services Manager	Coopted members

The work of SELIG has centred on establishing emotional literacy at the heart of the curriculum by carrying out a number of pilot projects in 12 schools, education services, and a multi-agency project. This work will be more fully described in Chapter 6: 'Emotional Literacy for local authorities'. SELIG has been engaged in producing Guidelines for Schools, Local Authorities, and Health Services on how to promote emotional literacy which will be published in 2001 to all Southampton schools and available nationally. This work arose from a shared conviction that educators in the public sector have a passionate commitment to making a difference for all children in our community.

The people who contributed to putting these guidelines together are unified by a common belief: namely, that emotional literacy is at least equal to other skills and competencies needed by children and young people, their parents, teachers, and those in the caring professions. At the core of the guidelines is the assertion that if teachers, pupils, parents, caring professionals, and others feel positive about themselves then they will learn more effectively. Put more succinctly:

Improving Emotional Literacy = Improving Standards
'Feel Good = Learn Good'

This hypothesis is currently under test and an independent evaluation of the first 18 months of our work has been completed by Professor Edmund Sonuga-Barke and Dr Robert Stratford of Southampton University. Again, this will be discussed in Chapter 6: 'Emotional Literacy for local authorities' and Chapter 7: 'Emotional Literacy may be the hard option'.

The Southampton guidelines for promoting emotional literacy include the following areas:

Introduction
Policy Development
Teaching and Curriculum
Staff (teachers, learning support assistants, and others in school)
Pupils
Parents
Governors

LEA, Social Services, Health
Emotionally Literate Society
Appendices (project pro-forma, resources, materials, National Emotional Literacy Interest Group, and weblinks).

My advice to readers is that even with the guidelines, each school needs to go through an iterative process looking at each of the areas above as experience suggests that whole-school ownership is otherwise jeopardised. So the areas covered by the guidelines need to be considered in conjunction with the documentation and practice associated with the human aspects of curriculum in Table 4.1, as a prelude to incorporating emotional literacy in the school development plan.

Promoting children's self-esteem... quality ingredients bake a better cake

Steven Stein (2000) pointed out that:

Low self-esteem may indeed be dysfunctional, but artificially high self-esteem may be almost as problematic. The child who learns the 'I am special' mantra without simultaneously building necessary life skills is done a tremendous disservice. Ladling out lavish and indiscriminate praise without making sure that you're helping the child actually achieve something that merits approval can lead to devastation when the world fails to continue to pat him or her on the back.

So the best advice for teachers is to make praise specific, targeted, real and deserved. It also means that every teacher needs to create regular opportunities for all children to actually earn praise, and that this is achieved through differentiating the curriculum appropriately and setting attainable goals, whether behavioural or attainment based.

In the section, 'Enhance your self-esteem' in Chapter 3, we described the necessity for us all to develop our own self-esteem and this is a pre-requisite for teachers trying to raise their pupils' self-esteem. The essence of success is to balance learning opportunities for children such that teachers can have legitimately high expectations matched to a child's current level of self-esteem. The table below (4.3) describes possible outcomes related to this precarious balancing act, and can help to inform teachers' choices regarding appropriate teaching and learning styles for individuals or groups of learners.

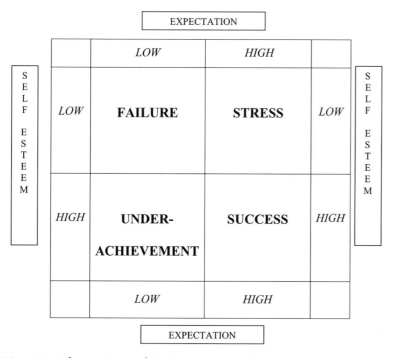

Table 4.3 The relationship between self-esteem and expectation (after Brighouse 2000)

The benefits to promoting self-esteem in a sustainable and meaningful way is that children will improve their attention span in response to being given attention, increase their levels of responsibility because they are being given an appropriate response, and become more achievement orientated because there are appropriately high levels of expectation. In addition, children are likely to become more understanding of others through better understanding themselves.

In planning how best to promote children's self-esteem we can make use of Michelle Borba's (1995) *Building Blocks of Self-Esteem*:

• Security
• Selfhood
• Affiliation (friendship)
• Mission (goals)
• Competence (ability).

Borba describes how low security is often indicated by stress, anxiety, and difficulty with change or new experiences, unsure of expectation and general distrust of others. In order to promote high security we can build trusting relationships, set reasonable limits that are consistently enforced and create a positive and caring environment.

Low selfhood is characterised by being uncomfortable with physical appearance, difficulty in accepting praise, high levels of conformity, and feelings of inadequacy. In order to foster high selfhood we can reinforce more accurate self-description, provide opportunities to discover the major sources of influence on the self, build an awareness of unique qualities, and enhance children's ability to express emotions effectively.

Low levels of affiliation (or inability to form friendships) is characterised by over-reliance on adult companions, isolation, over-dependence on objects, and poor understanding of the concept of friendship. In order to develop affiliation or friendship skills we can promote inclusion and acceptance in the group, provide opportunities to discover the interests and capabilities of others, develop social skills in forming friendships, and encourage peer approval through techniques such as 'circles of friends'.

Low levels of mission (goals or ambition) include indecisiveness, inability to see alternative views, poor task completion, poor self-evaluation skills, and poor goal-setting skills. We can improve mission by teaching decision-making skills, develop study skills including forward planning, and chart present and past academic and behavioural performances.

Low levels of competence are characterised by shyness, fear of making mistakes, inability to accept weaknesses, giving up easily, discounting success, and difficulty in identifying strengths. We can raise levels of personal competence by providing opportunities to increase awareness of competencies or strengths, teaching how to record progress and success, learning how to live with weaknesses and overcome them, and teaching the importance of self-praise.

For older children, particularly teenagers, Suzanne Harrill (1996) describes the features of high self-esteem as:

- Liking yourself
- Knowing yourself and only trying to be you
- Being kind to yourself and others
- Taking risks and learning new things
- Accepting yourself even if you want parts of you changed
- Honestly assessing your strengths and weaknesses without excessive pride or shame
- Taking responsibility for your own life
- Admitting when you have a problem
- Making amends if you have hurt someone
- Developing your talents and interests
- Balancing activities and quiet time
- Learning from your mistakes
- Standing up for yourself
- Loving being you
- Being willing to accept the consequences of your choices with regard to your thoughts, feelings and behaviours.

At first sight this list may seem over-ambitious, especially for any teacher (or parent) currently doing their best to raise or maintain the self-esteem of a teenager, but it represents an aim rather than a blueprint. We all feel low at times, but overall we need to feel that there is hope and that positive growth is possible.

Development proceeds through a series of ages and stages and, while it is true that the progression varies from individual to individual, there is some potential benefit to teachers and others in having knowledge of the broadly predictable trends within age ranges. We often talk of 'developmental milestones' and of the symbols associated with growing up: the first mouthful of solid food, the first step, the first word, the first tooth, and so on. Much less common is our collective understanding of emotional and social development, and there is little agreement about the veracity and genuine applicability of the 'staged models of emotional development'.

Ages and stages

Erik Erikson (1968) developed his theory which centred on a belief that there is a fixed and predetermined sequence to development. Erikson described an epigenetic principle that all development is dictated through genes that determine both stages and timing of the passage, and he called these psychosocial stages. He saw these stages as being universal and asserted that our socio-cultural environment also impacted on our development, and consequently the way we behaved. His so-called 'eight ages of man' (Table 4.4) were all characterised by a conflict, and expressed as a bipolar construct. The outcome of successful negotiation of a stage he held to be positive or adaptive, while a failure led to a negative or maladaptive outcome. He described this process more in terms of one outcome overriding another, rather than a linear 'either/or' outcome.

Stage	Crisis or conflict	Relationship	Outcome
0–1 year	Trust vs. Mistrust	Mother (now primary caregiver)	Trust and faith in others or mistrust
18 mths–3 years	Autonomy vs. Shame or Doubt	Parents	Self-control and self-assured, or self-doubt and fearful
3–5 years	Initiative vs. Guilt	Family	Purpose and direction, or loss of self-esteem
6–11 years	Industry vs. Inferiority	Neighbourhood and school	Competence in social skills, or failure to thrive
Adolescence 13–20 years	Identity vs. Role Confusion	Peers, out-groups, models of leadership	Sense of 'who I am', or uncertainty
Early adulthood 20 + years	Intimacy vs. Isolation	Partners in friendship, sex, competition, co-operation	Formation of enduring and meaningful relationships, or failure to love others
Middle age	Generativity vs. stagnation	Shared tasks with partner/family	Expansion of interests, caring for others, or turning in
Old age	Ego Integrity vs. Despair	'Mankind', 'My kind'	Satisfied with success and disappointment, or sense of failure and fear of death

Table 4.4 Erikson's eight stages of psychosocial development

Other important theories of emotional development include the developmental structural theory of Stanley Greenspan (1993), which considers the individual in terms of constitutional strengths and weaknesses, as well as what the individual then acquires or masters by building on inherited predisposition. Table 4.5 shows Greenspan's staged model of emotional development, and the resultant dangers or difficulties if a child fails to make the transition effectively from one stage to the next.

With regard to preschool education it follows from the theories of Erikson and Greenspan that nursery nurses, teachers, and other education staff should focus on teaching and learning styles that aim to promote emotional literacy particularly in regard to:

• Self-control
• Trust in educators
• Self-esteem
• Initiative.

In primary education the teachers and other staff consolidate preschool development and the emotional literacy focus should now be on:

• Promoting social competence
• Cultivating the ability to concentrate
• Learning to understand the importance of goals
• Developing friendship skills
• Developing children's ability to show empathy.

Stage	Age	Description of successful transition	Danger signs
First Stage	0–3 months	*Homeostasis:* taking an interest in the world, achieving a calm state necessary for learning	Hyper-excitable, easily overwhelmed or withdrawn and apathetic
Second Stage	2–7 months	*Attachment:* deep and rich multi-sensory relationship formed with primary caregiver	Lack of emotional responsiveness to people, especially primary caregiver
Third Stage	3–10 months	*Intentionality (Somatic-psychological differentiation):* learning to interact in back-and-forth reciprocal manner, via non-verbal messages	Minimal interaction, and non-verbal messages are erratic or not related to interaction with a significant other
Fourth Stage	9–24 months	*Behavioural Initiative and Organization:* forming a complex sense of the self, relating via coherent patterns and logical behaviour chains	Behaviour easily disrupted, going from one extreme behaviour to another without logical transition
Fifth Stage	18 months to 4 years	*Representational Elaboration:* child uses symbols and words to communicate feelings, ideas, intentions	Communication only by acting out, low impulse control, and poor distinction between fantasy and reality
Sixth Stage	4 years to adolescence	*Representational Differentiation:* emotional thinking develops, 'why' questions are posed to help express behavioural cause and effect	Lack of impulse control, inability to reflect on own behaviour or to accept and understand 'mixed feelings'

Table 4.5 Greenspan's stages of emotional development

Youngsters who have failed to acquire the skills above by the time of transition to secondary school may benefit from individual or group development work specifically geared at enhancing the likelihood of success in their more adult surroundings. Examples of such strategies are discussed in the next section of this chapter.

In order to nurture emotional literacy during secondary education, teachers and other school staff should focus on:

- Fostering the development of individual identity ('who am I?');
- Encouraging a longer term view of the student's role in life;
- Exploration of role (student, sibling, offspring, grandchild, friend, responsible young adult, citizen);
- Forming and maintaining stable relationships (friends, peers, teachers, parents);
- Empowering young people to ask 'why' questions and then learn to tolerate the ambiguity associated with feeling both good and bad feelings about the same thing or person (e.g. parents, teachers, school).

In young adulthood the emphasis is on the development of deep personal relationships, and failure to negotiate this stage well can result in isolation and ultimately deep depression and self-injurious behaviour or anti-social feelings acted out anger, aggression or violence.

It is important to acknowledge the crucial importance of parenting here, as clearly children who are developing well arrive at school at five years of age with highly sophisticated emotional and social skills. Children spend less than seven hours per day in school (see Figure 4.1), and then only for 39 weeks of the year, so this represents only 16 per cent per year of a child's life from the ages of 5–16 years (based on nine hours sleep per night). The quality of home-school partnership working is central to nurturing emotional literacy, and pivotal to any remediation programme for young people who have struggled to develop appropriately before getting to school. For a significant number of children the 46 per cent of time 'at home' may in fact be spent wholly unsupervised out on the streets, or left to their own devices with little parental interaction, supervision or encouragement. We will return to this debate in Chapter 5.

It is also salutary to consider that schools and local education authorities are held accountable for the development of emotional literacy, literacy, and numeracy while having only a third of the time to work with youngsters that parents have. Schools matter, and they matter a lot (Mortimore 1988, Rutter 1979, Reynolds 1992) and they can be highly influential in outcomes even against the odds (*Success Against The Odds*), but parents must surely have a greater responsibility than teachers to promote the emotional literacy of their children. The appropriate advice to teachers here is to have high expectations of what can be achieved in the promotion of emotional literacy at school, but to work smarter at fostering home-school partnerships even or especially with the hard-to-reach or challenging parents. Some of the issues, information, advice and

Percentage of time spent at school, home awake, and home asleep

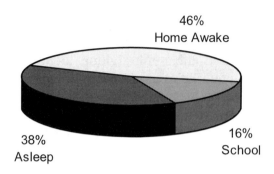

46%
Home Awake

38%
Asleep

16%
School

Figure 4.1   Percentage of time spent at school, home awake, and home asleep

guidance for parents in the next chapter are of direct relevance and application to teachers, particularly with regard to the nature and style of interaction and the needs of children in their most formative years.

Strategies and techniques

Many youngsters fail to make the progress described above, and even more show evidence of developmental delay in terms of their emotions. The number of children who become the subject of consultation between an educational psychologist and the school staff and/or parents in Southampton is approximately 15 per cent to 20 per cent of the school population, and the vast majority of these children have emotional and/or behavioural difficulties. Substantial numbers of children have problem anger that is expressed as verbal or physical hitting or hurting, and they can benefit from accessing 'Anger Management Groups'. Consequently, many local education authorities now have programmes in place to run anger management groups, and the best authorities have a systematic plan to train, develop, and empower school staff to take this work forward themselves.

The Southampton Anger Management Model (Faupel *et al.* 1998; Sharp and Herrick 2000), has been disseminated to representatives from over 45 local education authorities, and has been implemented in over 60 schools in Southampton alone. As well as anger management groups, other developmental group work centres on social skills training, building self-esteem, assertiveness training, anti-bullying initiatives and forming and maintaining friendships. As yet there is no other local education authority with a systematic three to five year programme to implement such work across all their schools, despite the evident and pressing need. Many teachers feel ill-equipped to manage challenging behaviour effectively, despite overhauling the school behaviour policy and even when trying very hard to 'catch children being good'. Consequently, we began our programme of anger management training and running anger management groups as part of a coordinated strategy to promote even better behaviour. This work began in earnest in 1995 with pilot groups, and twilight training sessions and grew into the production of a book, CD-ROM, video, and trainer's pack; all focused on anger management. The results of this work are encouraging both in terms of the outcomes for children and the systemic shift in schools mediated by teacher observers and co-workers.

Strong emotions can be quite frightening, and teachers need high quality training and development programmes in order to help children help themselves to manage their feelings more appropriately in a variety of settings. If educators hold both affective and cognitive education in high regard, then access to the curriculum will be promoted and this will support the drive for continuous improvement of standards in education.

Teachers have a key role to play in nurturing emotional literacy; their own and that of the children and young people who are the basis of success in all our futures. The alternative is a perpetuation of cycles of despair, and feelings of failure, impotence, and frustration that we cannot overcome the difficulties facing educators across the world.

If teachers are successful at nurturing emotional literacy then we will see:

- children who recognise and understand their feelings and so become more adept at handling and expressing them appropriately;
- children and teachers who will be less unduly stressed, and able to manage competing demands more effectively;
- children who will become better listeners, and more likely to see the other person's point of view;
- children who will improve their concentration and attention span and reduce their impulsivity;
- children who will have greater prowess at forming and maintaining relationships, and who will learn problem-solving skills that lead to enhanced interpersonal skills as adults;
- children who learn to manage conflicts and are therefore less likely to be involved in crime and particularly those crimes involving violence;
- children who will learn skills that enhance their future parenting skills.

This will only be possible if we adapt the environment to the child and stop pretending that all children can fit the environment, especially when that environment is a narrowly constrained 'one size fits all' curriculum. The successful school of the future is one where flexibility, high expectations, sophisticated pluralism, and tolerance are all in evidence in abundance.

Summary of Chapter 4: Emotional Literacy for teachers and learners

Emotional Literacy is acknowledged as of fundamental importance in educating children in a holistic and sustainable way.

Teacher Effectiveness research supports the need for understanding and using personal effectiveness strategies for improving the educative process.

Curriculum initiatives to nurture emotional literacy include taught curriculum schemes of work with explicit components of emotional literacy, and the caught or hidden curriculum that is fostered by having emotionally literate teachers and rich extra-curricular experiences.

Emotional Literacy Guidelines for Schools are to be published by Southampton City Council in 2001, but all LEAs could usefully consider how they nurture emotional literacy under the headings:

- Policy development
- Teaching and Curriculum
- Staff
- Pupils
- Parents
- Governors
- LEA, Social Services and Health
- Emotionally literate society.

Teachers can promote self-esteem by using strategies to foster the development of:

- Security
- Selfhood
- Friendship
- Goals
- Competence.

Ages and Stages of emotional and social development include the work of Erikson and Greenspan. Teachers can use these theories to underpin their practice so that children are given opportunities to recapitulate stages especially where they have failed to develop well and at an age-appropriate time.

Strategies and techniques to nurture emotional literacy include training and development in anger management, and the running of groups can reduce problem anger and reinforce social skills while raising self-esteem.

Action

1. Rate yourself as an educator on the following constructs:

- Demonstrating high expectations
  Low1 _____ 10 High

- Planning lessons
  Low 1_____ 10 High

- Using an extensive repertoire of teaching methods and strategies
  Low 1_____ 10 High

- Using ability to manage challenging behaviour in a humane but assertive way
  Low 1_____ 10 High

- Using time and resource management skills
  Low 1_____ 10 High

- Using assessment skills
  Low 1_____ 10 High

- Using sense of humour (mirthful and humane)
  Low 1_____ 10 High

- Showing empathy
  Low 1_____ 10 High

- Showing optimism
  Low 1_____ 10 High

2. Devise a brief plan for your personal development showing:

- What I intend to continue doing and do more or better:

- What I intend to reduce or stop doing:

- What I will do that is new:

3. Form a small group with two or three trusted colleagues and plan to have three meetings to discuss how you are nurturing emotional literacy:
a) your own (you have right to get your emotional needs met)
b) children's.

Chapter 5

Emotional Literacy for parents and carers

Your vision will become clear only when you can look into your own heart.

Carl Jung

The most crucial lesson I have learned as a parent, is that this is the most important job that I do. I have also realised that I would find it impossible to be a parent and nothing else. So to those full-time parents reading this I salute your patience, tenacity, and capacity to give so much of yourself. It is also worth noting that my job as parent is the only one I've had that did not require an application form, evidence of knowledge, skills, experience, and qualifications, and for which I have had no formal training or assessment of my competence. In every other job I do the accountability is high and performance management highly developed, but then, no one is paid to be a biological parent.

It is no surprise then that so many parents feel ill-equipped to be a good parent, and it is probably a testament to the resilience of children that so many of them thrive and succeed in life, despite and not because of their parenting. I suspect, however, that most parents are trying to do well most of the time, and that fundamentally most parents love their children even when they fail to parent effectively.

It would be more reasonable and realistic to expect and plan to be 'good enough parents' rather than the fantasy family with perfect parents, so often portrayed in advertisements and kitsch movies.

Good enough parents

The term 'good enough parent' was adapted by Bruno Bettelheim (1988) from Donald Winnicott's earlier concept of the 'good enough' mother. Essentially, Bettelheim argued that the pursuit of perfection as parent was as flawed as the hope that a child might be perfect. This also fits with a central tenet of rational emotive therapy, namely that we are all FHBs (Fallible Human Beings), and that it is our very fallibility that characterises the human condition. So we are all going to make mistakes as parents, and many of them, and thankfully children are able to cope with that provided we give generously and warmly of ourselves and create a relatively stable and secure relationship with our offspring.

Bettelheim wrote in 1988:

> Today, however, parents feel that much more is demanded of them if they are to raise their children successfully in a complicated world; moreover they are obliged to bear this responsibility without much prior experience.

He went on to describe how the emotional *and* physical distance separating generations made it less likely that young parents would look to their parents for advice on parenting, and that the consequence of this is that parents may even fear criticism if they seek advice. Taken together with the pace of change and development generally, Bettelheim argued that there is a new eagerness to seek 'expert' advice, and an over-reliance on science replacing an older wisdom inherent in tradition. The central message for parents is clear, reduce dependency on current orthodoxy or fashion from acclaimed 'experts' and learn to trust your intuition. By all means seek to make informed judgements by learning more about child development and incorporate views and theories about parenting that seem to work for you, but there are no rules for parenting, only views. My view is that the expression of love shown through the quality of sustained positive interaction between parents and children is the only fundamental need we should all aim to meet as parents, and the 'how to' is something that we each learn to do ourselves.

Berry Brazelton and Stanley Greenspan's (2000) book on the seven irreducible needs of children suggests that we need to address a massive range of issues and questions if children are to grow, learn and flourish. These include:

- Are parents spending enough time interacting with their children?
- How much time with parents do babies, toddlers, and older children need?
- In the case of child abuse or neglect, when should we fight to preserve the family?
- Is day care a massive social experiment that damages children?
- Should human development and childbirth education be part of every school curriculum?
- At what age can a child be separated from his or her primary caregivers overnight/ for a weekend/ for a week or two?
- In a divorce, will joint physical custody hurt a child?
- What guidelines should judges use for custody disputes?
- How much TV is too much TV?
- Is spanking child abuse?

None of the answers to the above are utterly clear-cut and non-controversial, but if our aim is to promote the emotional literacy of children then we clearly need to answer these and many other tough questions.

Type of Need	Description of need
The need for ongoing nurturing relationships	All babies need a warm, intimate relationship with a primary caregiver over years, not months or weeks. The best setting for this is at home with parents, and day care must change significantly if this is to be the source of such relationships.
The need for physical protection, safety, regulation	Both in the womb and in infancy, the environment should ensure protection from: physical and psychological harm; chemical toxins; exposure to violence.
The need for experiences tailored to individual differences	Every child has a unique biological make up and temperament, which means that experiences must be tailored to accommodate each child's nature if he or she is to achieve his or her potential.
The need for developmentally appropriate experiences	Children reach developmental stages at different ages, so they need to experience things at different rates. Too much or too little stimulation or unrealistic expectations can thwart development.
The need for limit setting, structure, and expectations	Children need structure and discipline, in order to progress to internal limit setting, channelling of aggression and ability to solve problems peacefully. They need incentive systems, not failure models.
The need for stable, supportive communities and cultural continuity	Children need a continuity of values in family, peer groups, religion, and culture as well as exposure to diversity.
The need to protect the future	Unless the previous six needs are met, and society makes these needs the highest priority, we will be jeopardising our children's future.

Table 5.1   The Seven irreducible needs of children – Brazelton and Greenspan (2000)

Frequently the answers will depend on who is asking the question, for example a single parent may have no option other than to return to work at the earliest opportunity following the birth of a son or daughter, but the question of the effect on the child still needs to be considered despite the practical imperative. There are powerful reasons for wanting to believe that babies and toddlers do not need their parent(s) for 8–10 waking hours per day (or more), and it may be deeply unfashionable to assert otherwise, but long-term emotional stability and maturity is not attainable with any certainty by having a series of primary caregivers throughout early infancy.

The government of Finland, who recently decided to increase paternity leave entitlement to several weeks, affords an example of a national answer to the question of the importance of fathers in early bonding and parenting, and maternity leave is also given prominence and for considerably longer in Scandinavia than other developed countries. Likewise there are progressive companies who recognise the need for parents to see their children during the day and so provide workplace crèches and nurseries, thereby at least making it possible for parents who have to work to see their children easily during their breaks.

Many questions concerning parenting and children's emotional literacy have serious financial implications for national economies, but it may be argued that the hidden costs of failing to recognise the benefits of family friendly policies may be found in delinquency rates, as well as crime and disorder statistics, not to mention the failure of youngsters to achieve their emotional and academic potential, and ultimately their ability to contribute as citizens and tax payers. What is needed are family friendly policies from national government that recognise the importance of quality parenting from parents not just paid carers.

Since life is messy, and we need to accept our current reality and make the best of it, then later to plan to improve the possibilities, let us consider some of the characteristics of a good enough parent:

- Makes good use of inner experience, as well as looking for advice from others which is carefully considered and not slavishly adhered to.
- Consistently uses praise, reinforcement, and has high expectations of their children and themselves.
- Imposes clear and reasonable boundaries, and follows through on consequences.
- Uses aversive consequences or punishment sparingly and in a humane way.
- Avoids physical punishment, since this is potentially misunderstood by children as a model of using force (or bullying) to get your needs met.
- Tries to talk so children will listen, and listen so children will talk.
- Explores dilemmas with children even at a very young age, and tries to use explanation and exploration much of the time.
- Encourages children to develop their own identity, even when their own identity is challenged.
- Allows children to make mistakes, and helps them to learn from them... but perhaps not immediately.
- Tells children they are special and valuable and backs this up by the quality of their actions and the nature of their relationship.
- Apologises sometimes when they get it wrong as a parent.
- Finds some time to play or simply to have fun.
- Recognises that they have their own needs and can't be perfect parents... or perfect in any way.

Clearly then, parenting is a process and being a good enough parent is a journey all parents are still on long after their children grow up. There is no blueprint for parenting, so any book or 'parent guru' that says 'follow my way and you can't go wrong' is best avoided. At best there are some ideas to consider before making choices and learning from our own mistakes.

Emotional coaching for children

As a good enough parent knows, it is very easy to tell children what to do and how to do it, but it is quite another thing to coach them. If coaching is taken as a process involving 'giving hints' and 'training' and perhaps even 'modelling', then the distinction between this and telling is that the aim is to allow the coached child to make their own choices and mistakes in the context of a safe and secure relationship. The strength of the concept of parent as coach pivots on the belief that most youngsters will tend to make good choices most of the time if given support, encouragement, and the information to make their choice.

If the fundamentally important first five years of life have been characterised by security, respect, encouragement and opportunity, then it is highly likely that a child will have very high self-esteem much of the time. Terri Apter (1997) argues:

> Children's self-esteem normally is not simply high or low. Instead it is like a layered cloud that undergoes daily shifts in shape and intensity, varying with a child's own mood, the familiarity of the setting, the task at hand, the attitudes of the people around her.

She goes on to describe how Stanley Coopersmith suggested that we imagine self-esteem as a kind of interior monologue a person holds – the self telling a story about the self. The significance of this is that the good enough parent will aim to support the establishment of a positive interior monologue, and as their child gets older they will help them to reaffirm their view of their capacity and capability to rise to challenges, even when they seem daunting.

A competent, caring coach is an effective communicator, and the good enough parent recognises the three basic styles of communication as described by Patrick Fanning and Matthew McKay (2000):

Passive Style

There is no direct expression of feelings, thoughts, and wishes. Frequently your own needs are subordinate to those of others, and passive listening or soaking up is a characteristic of how you appear. Passive speaking is often soft, weak and even wavering and may further be characterised by frequent pauses and hesitations.

Aggressive Style

Everything is stated up front, what is thought and felt, but often at the expense of others' rights and feelings. The appearance to others is of someone who is aloof, superior, and often blaming or hostile. There is an over-emphasis on absolute terms such as 'always' or 'never', and little tolerance of ambiguity.

Assertive Style

Characterised by direct statements regarding feelings, thoughts, and wishes while taking account of the needs of others. Listening is attentive and communication checks are frequent, but not at the expense of your own rights and dignity. An assertive communicator can give and receive compliments, and does not usually react defensively or with hostility to criticism especially if it appears constructive or justified.

So the good enough parent will tend to use an assertive communication style as part of their preferred way of being, and this strengthens their role as emotional coach. Paul Coleman (2000) describes the features of an emotional coach as Smart Talk: The Six Ways We Speak To Our Kids, and this is summarised by the mnemonic TENDER communication:

T – Teaching
E – Empathising
N – Negotiating
D – Do's and Don'ts
E – Encouraging
R – Reporting

Teaching is most effective when couched in terms like 'Let me explain…' or 'Watch how I do it, then you try…' or 'How did you get to that?' usually with the emphasis on letting the learner have a say in whether teaching is what they want or need at that point.

Empathising is most useful when a child is experiencing strong or overwhelming emotions, and that is also when it is hardest to do! For example, if a child is angry then the parent receives some of that anger and we often respond by projecting it back. A better empathic response would be to acknowledge the feeling and leave a space for the child to think, for example by saying: 'You seem really fed up about that… is that right?'

Negotiating is perhaps over-used by parents and can lead to unnecessary protracted arguments, this is because many parents begin negotiation when they never intended to concede or compromise, for example over bedtime or coming-in time. A more honest response might be: 'I cannot agree to that during the week, but I am prepared to relax bedtime at the weekend.' An example of negotiation over say bedroom mess might sound like: 'I know you've already done quite a lot of tidying up, is there anything special you'd like to do later when you've finished?'

Do's and Don'ts should be reserved for those times when there needs to be unequivocal clarity of expectation, and most 'don'ts' can be reframed into 'do's' so that young children experience a more positive communication than a long negative list of rules. For example: 'I need you to keep your feet off the furniture when you've got shoes on' instead of 'Don't climb on the furniture'. In the interests of safety there are times when an abrupt 'Don't' is called for, but if over-used it will likely go unheeded, e.g. 'Don't cross' when about to step off the pavement into traffic, but even this could be reframed to 'Stop, and look both ways'.

Encouraging is the basic quality or feature of emotional coaching for children of all ages. Praising effort, self-control, thoughtful gestures, and indeed any desirable behaviour will result in children feeling good about themselves.

Reporting is a technique that is more neutral than the others above, and includes statements of fact, common questions, simple expressions of feeling, and requests. If used in a more directive way then it can support dialogue, for example: 'Tell me about what you enjoyed at school today.'

If we combine these communication techniques with a series of steps then we have a strategy for emotional coaching. John Gottman (1997) describes the Five Key Steps for Emotion Coaching as:

1. Being aware of the child's emotion;
2. Recognising the emotion as an opportunity for intimacy and teaching;
3. Listening empathetically and validating the child's feelings;
4. Helping the child verbally label the emotions; and
5. Setting the limits while helping the child problem solve.

As parents we will have an inevitable struggle to do the right thing, even when we think we know what that is, and we have more chance of enjoying this process if we learn to forgive ourselves as well as our children when things don't turn out as we'd hoped. Emotional coaching for young children is more likely to be successful if we just build the principles above into our psyche and later our behavioural repertoire, rather than fuss about following a process exactly.

Emotional coaching for teenagers

The principles for emotional coaching are the same for children of all ages, but adolescence is a period of development that many parents *and* teenagers experience as very challenging both individually and collectively. The term 'adolescence' is rooted in the Latin *adolescere* meaning *'to grow to maturity'*, and in emotional development terms this is a crucial period as the young person struggles to come to terms with very powerful feelings. Adolescence is described by many authors as a period of *storm and stress* and broadly occurs during the teen years, though there is some variation as biological adolescence can begin before the teen years or end beyond them. Interestingly the term 'teenager' was only coined in 1953 and Montemayor's research (1983) indicates that adolescence has changed very little despite enormous social and economic changes, but he also described how parents and adolescents are in conflict: 'All families some of the time, and some families all of the time.'

Emotional coaching for teenagers requires an understanding of the developmental tasks that an adolescent needs to work through. Jean Clarke and Connie Dawson (1998) describe these tasks:

- To take more steps toward independence;
- To achieve a clearer emotional separation from the family;
- To emerge gradually, as a separate, independent person with own identity and values;
- To be competent and responsible for own needs, feelings and behaviours;
- To integrate sexuality into the earlier developmental tasks.

Clarke and Dawson also note that adolescence involves revisiting or recycling tasks of earlier stages – being, doing, thinking, identity and power, and structure – with new information and with the sometimes-confusing pressures of their emerging sexuality. Which may explain why teenagers can act very grown up or highly immature by turn. So when you're trying to be a good enough emotional coach for your teenage children here are some of the things Clarke and Dawson suggest you try to do:

Affirm your teenagers for trying to get things right most of the time.
Accept your children's feelings and try to be open to dialogue about their sexual feelings if they choose to discuss them.
Confront unacceptable behaviour.
Be clear about your stance on drugs, smoking and sexual behaviours.
Identify the ways your teenager is becoming separate and support their newfound independence.
Understand and support your teenager's reworking of tasks from earlier developmental stages.
Accommodate your teenager's new identity even though it may mean compromising parental expectations or dreams for your child.
Celebrate the adolescent's growing up and welcome to adulthood.

Conversely there are a number of behaviours that are best avoided, even though it may be difficult, including:

Rigid rules or no rules or refusal to negotiate rules.
Unresponsive or uncaring behaviour.
Cruel teasing for example about interests, fantasies, dreams, sexuality.
Failure to confront self-injurious behaviour from drugs to eating or sleeping problems.

Maintaining a dependency relationship instead of allowing move to separation.

Ultimately the period of late adolescence is a time for adjusting to the emergence of your child as an adult, and this is always going to be a big challenge. The core skill for being an emotional coach with a young adult is showing tolerance of their struggle and avoiding unnecessary conflict. John Gottman (1997) asserts that it is important to show respect for teenagers, and this will involve communicating your values but in a non-judgemental way and briefly rather than through boring and tedious lectures or telling-offs. He also points out that finding the right level of involvement in your teenager's life is one of the toughest challenges you face, and it may be that the teenager will begin to take the lead in deciding what that balance looks like.

If teenagers have had emotional coaching through their early years and their parents are of the good enough variety, then it is likely that conflict will occur some of the time, but not all or even most of the time. I would like to challenge the perverse view that appears to predominate that teenagers *have to be* difficult – we're all difficult at times but age is not the only predisposing factor. It is also important to work on resolution of conflict, especially when a blow-up has occurred, but that is best done when all parties are back on planet earth and not in the heat of the moment.

Getting to 'Yes'

The process of emotional coaching is essentially about principled negotiation as described above, and in an entirely different context, namely business dispute mediation, this is what Roger Fisher and William Ury wrote about over a decade ago in their book called *Getting To Yes*. In their view the first rule of principled negotiation is separating relationship issues (or 'people problems') from substantive issues, and dealing with them independently. They go on to describe one kind of 'people problem' as being the fact that people see or define a situation differently, depending on who they are and what their situation is. Fisher and Ury may have a different starting point than a good enough parent, in that parents may choose to try and understand relationship problems at the same time as substantive issues, but in *Getting To Yes* they offer a potentially very useful framework for parents and their children to use in obtaining a *better-for-both outcome* when disputes arise. The seven strategies for treating perception problems, and hence for emotional coaching, may be summarised for parents as follows:

First, try to see the situation through your children's eyes, without necessarily agreeing with their perception, but by trying to understand what and why they think and feel as they do.

Second, don't deduce your children's intentions based on your own fears, but rather offer a generous interpretation or keep an open mind.

Third, avoid blaming your children for any problem, so adopt a 'no blame' culture, and give them the benefit of the doubt.

Fourth, talk about each other's perceptions, and acknowledge any points of overlap and common ground and build on these.

Fifth, seek opportunities to act inconsistently with your children's misperceptions, which means do not say or do things that confirm your children's worst fears. Instead say or do things that can be interpreted positively whenever possible, so that you 'disappoint their negative or inaccurate perception' of you.

Sixth, give your children a stake in the outcome by making sure they participate in the negotiation process, even when they are quite young. Also try to foster ownership of the process by your children and help them to come to trust that this is the usual way you do things.

Seventh, whatever you propose should be consistent with your children's principles and self-image, so that they do not feel their integrity is compromised. For young children this simply means helping them to build a positive self-image and for older teenagers it means some compromise on your part if they challenge your value system.

Whenever there's a real or potential dispute then the nature and quality of interaction between parent and child needs to be principled, intentionally positive and aiming for a 'better-for-both outcome'. Other authors characterise this in terms of winning or losing as set out in Table 5.2, but this may be an unnecessary bipolarisation if the 'better-for-both' recognises that one may 'win' more than the other, but both have a positive outcome.

CONSIDERATION	HIGH	Lose/Win	Win/Win
	LOW	Lose/Lose	Win/Lose
		LOW	HIGH
		COURAGE	

Table 5.2   Outcomes from interaction:
Aiming for Win/Win=Better-for-both

If as a parent I am very considerate of my children and I have the courage of my convictions, then there is a good chance of a 'win/win' outcome, though it needs to be acknowledged that children, particularly when young, have a limited understanding of compromise. There is considerable scope for accruing interest in your children's 'emotional bank account' if just occasionally you let them win, and they know about it. The good enough parent trying to be emotionally literate and trying to coach their youngsters may have their patience and tenacity tested to the limit every time this dynamic is in operation.

Overcoming setbacks and coping with reality

I took leave from work one day to get some of this chapter written, and in the afternoon I went to collect my daughters from their schools, a rare treat for me and a surprise for them. While waiting outside the school, with my head full of emotional coaching, I overheard a little preschooler say excitedly to her mum standing at the school gate:

'Can I play with Sharon tonight mum, can I?'
Her mum replied: 'Shut up I'm trying to think!'
Undeterred the little girl said: 'Yes, but can I play?'
Mum said: 'I told you to shut up, now shut up or I'll hit you!'

This was a rude return to one kind of reality, a sad and all too prevalent example of a parent who may operate differently at other times, but who on this occasion was clearly not able to aim for a better-for-both outcome. The vast majority of parents who read this book will undoubtedly start from a different baseline, namely wanting to help their children succeed and looking for helpful and wholesome ways to do that. Even so we all lose our cool sometimes, or say or do things we know are hurtful to our children, so this section is about learning from experience so that we keep trying to do our best.

Rob Bocchino (1999) describes learning from experience as 'self-coaching' and quotes Albert Einstein as having defined insanity as 'doing the same thing over and over again, but expecting a different outcome.' In the context of the feeling or affective domain, others refer to this repetitive behaviour as the re-enactment of a script learned in the family and oft repeated, despite the negative consequences and even a desire to change. Bocchino goes on to emphasise the connection between continuous learning, continuous improvement, and the learning cycle (experience > process > hypothesise > test/use > experience and so on), and says that outstanding performance is related to meta-cognition (the ability to think about thinking). I suggest that combining meta-cognition with feelings has the potential to help us more in our effort to improve both our own and our children's emotional literacy.

As parents we can get into self-coaching, in order to overcome setbacks and cope with our messy reality, by following a four-step learning cycle:

1. Observe and record our experience, noting (mentally, or more reliably by use of a diary or journal) what works and what doesn't in relation to our feelings first about our self and later in our role as parent.
2. Think about the experience, and process this over time by reading and re-reading our diary.
3. Form a best guess or hypothesis about the best way to handle our feelings and thoughts.
4. Test out our best guess or hypothesis and then reflect on the outcome.

Bocchino (1999) suggests that the learning cycle operates best when we have the *attitude of a learner*, which involves us in questioning what we know or challenging what we think we know… so that we see our experiences through fresh eyes. Our ultimate goal is to regularly apply this attitude and approach in order to see our lives as a rich set of experiences that we can learn from. If we adopt this approach as adults, and in role as parents, then it is highly likely that our children will try it too, and in so doing our self-coaching informs our ability to act as emotional coach for our children.

One way to confront a harsh reality, for example when we get it horribly wrong and shout at our children having lost our cool, is to return to our vision of where we want to be. Bocchino's definition of vision can help us here: Vision of our self as emotional coach is future oriented, stated in the positive, concrete and specific, within our sphere of influence, and systemic (fits our overall aims for our self). In practice this means that when we hit an obstacle, like losing our temper, then we go round it, over it, through it, or just avoid it next time. There is merit in sharing our struggle with our children, so tell them when you're finding it hard, but be clear that you know it is your responsibility to do something about it.

Some of the features of a parent acting as an emotional coach and coping with reality are summarised by Gottman (1997):

• Values the child's negative emotions as an opportunity for intimacy;
• Can tolerate spending time with a sad, angry, or fearful child;
• Is aware of and values his or her emotions;
• Sees the world of negative emotions as an important arena for parenting;
• Is sensitive to the child's emotional states;
• Is not usually confused or anxious about the child's emotional expression;
• Respects the child's emotions;
• Does not poke fun at negative feelings;
• Does not say how the child should feel;
• Does not feel they have to fix every problem for the child;
• Uses emotional moments to listen, empathise, help label emotions, offer guidance, set limits, and teach problem-solving skills.

Now this list can feel persecutory, because none of us is able to keep this up all of the time, so our reality is that this is an aim that we recognise is attainable only some of the time. Liking ourselves as parents, faults and all, can help us to aim high and in turn to help our children feel they can do that too. The final word on emotional literacy for parents and carers should be... enjoy it, the rewards can be fantastic!

Summary of Chapter 5: Emotional Literacy for parents and carers

Bettelheim's 'Good Enough Parent' is one who recognises that the pursuit of perfection as parent is as flawed as the hope that a child might be perfect.

Greenspan's Seven Irreducible Needs of Children:

1. The need for ongoing nurturing relationships;
2. The need for physical protection, safety, regulation;
3. The need for experiences tailored to individual differences;
4. The need for developmentally appropriate experiences;
5. The need for limit setting, structure, and expectations;
6. The need for stable, supportive communities and cultural continuity;
7. The need to protect the future.

Emotional coaching for children:
Coleman's Ways to speak to children:

T – Teaching
E – Empathising
N – Negotiating
D – Do's and Don'ts
E – Encouraging
R – Reporting

Gottman's Five Steps for emotional coaching:

1. Being aware of the child's emotion;
2. Recognising the emotion as an opportunity for intimacy and teaching;
3. Listening empathetically and validating the child's feelings;
4. Helping the child verbally label the emotions; and
5. Setting the limits while helping the child problem solve.

Emotional coaching for teenagers:
Clarke and Dawson tasks –

- To take more steps toward independence;
- To achieve a clearer emotional separation from the family;
- To emerge gradually, as a separate, independent person with own identity and values;
- To be competent and responsible for own needs, feelings and behaviours;
- To integrate sexuality into the earlier developmental tasks.

Getting to 'Yes':
Aim for a *better–for–both* outcome by trying to see through their eyes, give the benefit of the doubt, adopt a 'no blame' culture, discuss your views, disappoint their negative perceptions, give a stake in the outcome, and be consistent with your children's values.

Coping with reality: Adopt a learning cycle = experience > process > hypothesise > test/use > experience and so on.

Action

Keep a 'parent' diary:

Day	Feelings	Thoughts	Actions	Future ideas

Use these headings to follow the four steps of the **learning cycle:**

1. Observe and record our experience, noting (mentally, or more reliably by use of a diary or journal) what works and what doesn't in relation to our feelings first about our self and later in our role as parent.
2. Think about the experience, and process this over time by reading and re-reading our diary.
3. Form a best guess or hypothesis about the best way to handle our feelings and thoughts.
4. Test out our best guess or hypothesis and then reflect on the outcome.

Talk to your children about what you're trying to do in simple, honest, and concrete terms.

Discuss how this is going to impact on your parenting practice with your partner if you have one, or your parent or a trusted friend if you don't have a partner.

Buddy-up with another parent who is a kindred spirit and support each other in trying to be an emotional coach.

Ask your local parent partnership officer (call the local education authority) to set up a parent support group to look at promoting emotional literacy.

Chapter 6

Emotional Literacy for local authorities

It is one of the most beautiful compensations of this life that no man can sincerely try to help another without helping himself.
                                                        Ralph Waldo Emerson

Many local authorities are so busy trying to meet statutory duties that they may be slow to recognise the value and importance of emotional literacy for their citizens, and indeed for their workforce. Local authorities have become increasingly accountable in recent years, both through deliberate modernisation and because of inspection, audit and public scrutiny. It is no surprise then that imagination and creativity are not the first words associated with strategic planning in local authorities, especially since they have become increasingly insecure places to work and are facing what often seems like open hostility from central government irrespective of political colour. Tighter budgets and ever increasing delegation could potentially restrict any real innovation across a whole city or county as we all pursue the current craze of 'more for less'. Even so, there are a few local authorities that have encouraged thinking and planning that is 'out of the box' and have supported work that considers changes ranging from the 'mild to the wild'.

Local government reorganisation during the late 1990s led to the establishment of many more local authorities, and some of the new unitary authorities were characterised by a 'can do' attitude that is more open to challenging old orthodoxies and a new energy directed at finding better ways to work in order to improve the quality of life both for their residents and employees. Southampton City Council is one such authority, and the strategy for promoting emotional literacy serves as an example of good practice for other authorities, some of it directly replicable and other parts which may simply not fit the host culture or climate of another authority.

A strategy for promoting emotional literacy

The emotional literacy strategy in Southampton arose from a shared conviction that educators in the public sector have a passionate commitment to making a difference for all children in our community, irrespective of ability, socio-economic background, gender, or race. The people who devised this strategy are further unified by a common belief: namely that emotional literacy is at least equal to other skills and competencies needed by children and young people, their parents, teachers, and those in the caring professions. The strategy seeks to put back the humanity into the educative process that has been lost by an over-focus solely on attainment.

At the heart of the strategy is a vision that the young people of Southampton will become adult citizens who are able to recognise, understand, handle, and appropriately express their emotions. Growing out of this vision there are a number of specific objectives, and each of these can be task analysed to give sub-objectives that contribute to the realisation of the vision. The objectives include:

- To place emotional literacy at the heart of the curriculum (identifiable in all lessons and school activities).
- To promote insight into the emotional factors in learning (for teachers, parents, children and others).
- To support teachers in meeting their needs (recognising that they cannot promote emotional literacy for children if they are themselves emotionally and physically exhausted).
- To promote inclusion and obviate the need for any kind of exclusion (ultimately this should also apply to disciplinary exclusion).
- To share good practice in schools, education services, multi-agency teams, and across the city in order to further promote emotional literacy.
- To carry out action research so as to promote evidence based practice in and beyond education.
- To raise standards for all children both in terms of their emotional literacy and attainment.
- To establish productive partnerships beyond education to promote emotional literacy (e.g. police, trusts, theatre, film, etc.).
- To develop democracy in schools to mirror the role we want young people to fulfil on becoming adult citizens.
- To define emotionally literate learners and identify how to help make that happen.
- To develop curriculum materials (age/stage specific) to support the work in schools.
- To develop a resource bank (measures, references, materials).
- To develop year on year measurements for assessing progress (e.g. Southampton Emotional Literacy Scales (SELS) for individuals and institutions).

It is recognised that there are some serious tensions inherent in the list of objectives above, for example the juxtaposition of the standards and inclusion agenda. Few educators or parents will have serious objections to the core principle of inclusion… namely that all children should have a right to receive a good education local to their home and irrespective of their individual ability, special need, race, gender or religion. However, many people have objections to implementing this ahead of a major national initiative to skill up staff, resource at the appropriate levels, and reassure parents of the school's ability to be inclusive. Even more people have concerns about the ability of schools to achieve this within existing resources and current competency levels of teachers and other staff, and some make the false assumption that inclusion may inevitably lower standards. Clearly inclusion without training, resources and national commitment may well impact adversely on standards, so an emotionally literate national government would not plan to promote inclusion without a well thought through plan to make it successful.

Most local authorities are trying to make inclusion a reality, but we need a more coherent stance from central government that currently adopts a position that you can promote inclusion while planning to retain segregated special schools. Further confusion has been created by the 'have your cake and eat it' line from central government that says permanent exclusions have to fall, but that some pupils (such as persistent bullies) need to be excluded. Simply consider the destructive apartheid policies that endured for so long in South Africa, and I believe we will come to hold segregationist schooling policies in the same regard in the years to come. Already few people believe that children should be segregated simply because they rely on a wheelchair for mobility, but children with emotional and behavioural difficulties are viewed with open hostility by many educators. A far-sighted government would articulate a policy that recognises the need for a 10- to 15-year plan to provide the resources, training, curriculum, and appropriate spaces and buildings in the mainstream setting to accommodate *all* children.

An emotionally literate school is one that recognises the value and importance of inclusion and spends time on seeking effective solutions to make it possible rather than the emotionally illiterate school that seeks to find all the reasons why not to promote inclusive education. Having said that, all schools deserve to have the tools to do the job, the right encouragement, and the appropriate support both from their local authority and from central government.

Developing an emotional literacy strategy: Steps to success

Some of these are described in Sharp (2000) and Sharp and Herrick (2000).

Step 1

Establish a partnership based on common interest in emotional literacy involving at least two senior officers of the LEA or local authority. In Southampton this partnership comprises Ian Sandbrook (Chief Inspector) and myself. We began our exploration by sharing our completed life maps and learned more about each other in one hour than during the previous 11 years of working together. This led to a genuine understanding and fuller collaboration between psychologists, inspectors and later other officers too.

Step 2

Begin with the individual so that the whole process is built on each of us exploring our own emotional literacy, firstly by life mapping (described earlier in this book) and later by measurement of your emotional quotient (EQ). The essence of this work is the reflective and introspective nature of the move towards improving emotional literacy, and based on the belief that it is inappropriate, and less likely to be successful, if we try to promote other people's emotional literacy if we are not actively trying to work on our own development.

Over 1,200 people in Southampton have now completed life maps, and for many this was the first time that they had formally reflected on their 'journey so far', prompting some very significant changes. Many people say that the life mapping helps them to regain a sense of perspective and proportion, and gives them a little time 'to stand and stare' as W.H. Davies termed it. This process of reflection has often led to a reappraisal of the endless 'working harder and longer', rather than trying to find ways to be more effective as educators while having a life beyond work.

Step 3

Plan an awareness-raising programme of seminars, presentations and publications for head teachers, governors, parents, pupils, police, and colleagues in health, social services and employers in the city or county.

In Southampton we invited all head teachers to an introductory seminar and were thrilled to welcome well over 80 per cent of them to our open meetings, and for the evaluations of the events to be so universally positive. This programme was later extended to all education managers, and then to deputy head teachers, followed by other colleagues both in and beyond education. By December 2000 the introductory seminar or presentation had been run for a total of over 1,000 teachers across the city, and for 125 governors, plus 90 colleagues in health and social services, and 30 community liaison police officers. Clearly, there are capacity issues for rolling out a programme of this nature, and we learned from experience that more delivery time needed to be planned-in for such a significant citywide strategy.

Step 4

Publish widely that emotional literacy is a primary priority, ranked on a par with literacy and numeracy and embed this prominently in the authority's Education Development Plan. Obviously there are resource issues to be incorporated, primarily people, and also funds, books, videos, CD-ROMs, and training.

The Strategic Education Plan for Southampton goes well beyond the statutory requirement for an education development plan and incorporates the ideal to make Southampton THE City of Learning; one major contributory factor to attaining this will be to promote emotional literacy for the children, parents, citizens and employees of Southampton. Some of the funding has come from core service time, some from school improvement monies, some from Standards funds, and some from trusts and foundations.

Step 5

Establish an Emotional Literacy Interest Group with a diverse range of people chosen from a wide variety of stakeholder groups or interested parties from across the authority. Plan a series of meetings across at least a year, and invest time in agreeing a common agenda and later the process for working together.

Southampton Emotional Literacy Interest Group (SELIG) was established in early 1998 and both the representation and the agenda for the first two years' work is described earlier in Chapter 4. Attendance at the meetings has been higher than for any other task or working group I have been on, and I think the spirit of working has been more positive too, helped a little by our decision to have high quality refreshments for every meeting as members generously give up their early evenings to achieve our goals.

Step 6

Demonstration or pilot projects should be undertaken in schools, the LEA, and in multi-agency settings. The purpose of these is to establish what can be achieved in reality and to ground the work in observable settings, particularly so that others (e.g. schools, other LEAs) can begin to see how the theory meets practice. These projects are best commissioned using a standard pro-forma that includes: project statement, objectives, resources, outcome measures, and so on, as set out in Table 6.1 Emotional Literacy Projects (p.81).

Southampton Emotional Literacy Interest Group (SELIG) set 12 projects running in 1999, of which 10 are school based (one ceased as key staff left the school), one is focused on Education Services, and one is a multi-agency project involving education, health, and social services. The titles of these projects are given below:

1. An intervention to improve self-esteem in a selected group of pupils: Primary School.
2. An intervention to encourage friendship skills among unpopular children: Primary School.

3. To develop emotionally literate staff and pupils through a whole school, curricular initiative to help pupils develop and use an appropriate 'feelings' vocabulary: Primary School.

4. An intervention to increase self-esteem in two children selected because of their disruptive behaviour: Junior School.

5. An intervention for Mid-day Supervisory Assistants (MDSAs) aimed at raising their self-esteem and acculturating them into the school's emotional literacy ethos: Two Infant Schools working together.

6. An intervention for the parents of adolescent children with anger management problems: Comprehensive School for Girls.

7. An intervention to develop appropriate assertiveness in certain pupils (probable targets for bullying), to increase their attendance at school: Mixed Comprehensive School.

8. To develop an emotional literacy curriculum package for Year 7; to develop skills in teachers to deliver the curriculum; to help staff develop EL abilities; to liaise with feeder schools and coordinate joint strategies for EL promotion, including parent workshops and EL support for Year 5 provided by Year 8 pupils: Mixed Comprehensive School.

9. To promote more effective and emotionally literate communication between the agencies concerned with individual children and young people: Multi-agency project (Behaviour Resource Service with joint funding and management) involving social workers, psychiatrists, psychologists, and others.

10. To assess the emotional literacy of officers in education services, to then promote increased EL in order to improve efficiency and effectiveness: All the managers in education (22 people) including Director, Assistant Directors and all of the next tier of management. Further description of this work appears in Chapter 7 and the completed project pro-forma is to be found in the appendices.

Emotional Literacy Interest Group

1. School/Agency:

   Address:

   Phone: Fax: e-mail:

2. Project Statement

3. Project Director:

   Post (e.g. Head / Dep H/T / PEP):

   Contact phone: e-mail:

4. Project Objectives

5. Work undertaken to promote a shared understanding of Emotional Literacy:

   a)   Definition

   b)   How objectives are to be achieved

   c)   How project contributes to wider EL aims

Table 6.1   Southampton Emotional Literacy Projects — Pro-forma

6. What benchmarks have you got before project started?

Hard data: (Quantitative)

Soft data: (Qualitative)

7. What improvements are you hoping to see

a)   Directly

b)   Indirectly

as a result of undertaking this work?

8. What have you done to link policies on

- learning and achievement

- behaviour and discipline

- health promotion

- PSHE

- spiritual, moral and cultural development

- equal opportunities

- citizenship

- social inclusion

- crime and disorder?

9. How does your project help to 'establish emotional literacy at the heart of the curriculum'?

Table 6.1   Southampton Emotional Literacy Projects — Pro-forma

| 10. | Where does this work fit in to your development plan? (Quote extracts if applicable.) |

| 11. | Can you produce evidence to show that promoting emotional literacy raises standards? |

| 12. | Have you produced some examples of good practice to share with colleagues? |

| 13. | How does this all fit in with the notion of continuous improvement – can we do better and feel better? |

| 14. | What has not worked to promote emotional literacy? (e.g. learning point from a project that has not worked as you hoped) |

Table 6.1 Southampton Emotional Literacy Projects — Pro-forma

PROMOTING EMOTIONAL LITERACY:

'People are able to recognise, understand, handle,
and appropriately express their emotions.'

Aiming to
'establish emotional literacy at the heart of the curriculum.'

Step 7

Evaluation of implementation of emotional literacy strategy should be planned in from the outset, and preferably involving external evaluators for more reliable validation of the work. So many initiatives are begun without planning how to assess their success and the consequences could outweigh the costs, so this needs to be budgeted for both in terms of money and people's time.

Southampton was successful in securing financial support (£10,000) from the Calouste Gulbenkian Foundation in order to engage external consultants to undertake the evaluation of Phase 1 of our emotional literacy strategy, and extracts from their report are included later in Chapter 7 ('Emotional literacy for education'). The Southampton emotional literacy strategy comprises three planned phases:

Phase 1: 1998–2000   Introduction, awareness-raising, seminars, demonstration and pilot projects, and independent evaluation of Phase 1.

Phase 2: 2000–2002   Dissemination and Implementation of Emotional Literacy Guidelines for Schools, continuation of existing projects, new set of projects to involve another cohort of schools, extension of emotional literacy across other City Council directorates, evaluation of Phase 2.

Phase 3: 2002–2004   Dissemination and implementation of Emotional Literacy Guidelines in all schools across the city, develop Southampton as The City Of Learning and working towards being the emotionally literate city, evaluation of Phase 3.

Step 8

Incorporate emotional literacy strategy in all major plans including the Education Development Plan, Behaviour Support Plan, Early Years Plan, Connexions, etc. This needs to become a cross-cutting strategy that permeates all areas of work, and eventually becomes a part of the fabric of the way we do business. Action research is also needed to investigate the hypothesis that promoting emotional literacy leads to raising of standards of attainment, and considerable work will be needed to identify any direct or indirect links. It will be even more difficult, but worthwhile, to try and investigate causality, and especially so that resources may be targeted more effectively in order to support children's development.

I suspect that one reason why this work has been so well received in over 30 LEAs that have purchased training, development, and consultancy from Southampton, is that this is non-statutory and has no three line whip from central government. The warm reception for this work comes from the fact that many, if not most, people in local authorities are value driven and actually *want to make a difference* for children and families, and emotional literacy resonates with that ambition. However, there is a pressing need for this work to gain national endorsement and become embedded in education policy.

Michael Barber (2000), Head of the Standards and Effectiveness Unit of the Department for Education and Employment (DfEE), argues that we need to understand and transform the ways in which children learn, and that this is crucial to raising standards. He also argues that teaching thinking skills in a disciplined way will have a positive effect on raising standards, and he said: 'Related to the work on thinking skills is the development of strategies to enhance emotional literacy…' and went on to describe the work in Southampton as an example of this in action, and to assert that together this will contribute to better citizenship and a more socially inclusive society. So clearly there is awareness in the DfEE of the importance of this work, and some politicians in government were supportive of the work to promote emotional literacy while in the shadow cabinet.

Collectively we need to establish a national recognition of the potential value of promoting emotional literacy, and to embed this at the heart of the curriculum. To this end the reader is encouraged to join Antidote: The Campaign for Emotional Literacy, and to contribute both at a local and a national level. In February 2001 Antidote published a Manifesto calling for a society that is able to handle the richness of its emotional life, and each of us can then decide how best to contribute to that agenda.

Antidote: 5th Floor, 45 Beech Street, London EC2Y 8AD

Fax 020 – 7588 – 4900   Tel 020 – 7588 – 5151
www.antidote.org.uk   *emotionalliteracy@antidote.org.uk*

In addition, the National Emotional Literacy Interest Group (NELIG) has been established and it aims to become *the* resource for educators trying to promote emotional literacy. A website has been established at *http://www.nelig.com* that will become an indispensable resource for all of us involved in education as people contribute to it over the coming months and years. The site is under development but currently comprises:

- Welcome.
- Introduction.
- Founding Friends of nelig.com.

- Friends and contributors of nelig.com.
- Presentations (e.g. PowerPoint presentations for use in schools and with other groups).
- Papers (published elsewhere or exclusively on nelig.com).
- Annotated Resource Section (Giving people details of books, videos, CD-ROMs, puppets, games and other resources with evaluative comments from people who have used them in their work).
- Discussion Forum (Cyber dialogue forum for educators to discuss their work, views, ideas, hopes and fears in regard to emotional literacy. The Calouste Gulbenkian Foundation is generously supporting the development of this site... so use it or lose it! We intend to have a steady stream of contributions from around the country and later to make NELIG a more international site and so metamorphose into ELIG: *The Emotional Literacy Interest Group.*
- Web links... hyperlinks to other sites of interest to educators or parents involved in promoting emotional literacy.

The nurture committee for nelig.com currently includes representatives from the LEAs of:

- Southampton
- Bristol
- Portsmouth
- Birmingham
- Cumbria;

We can use the networking through nelig.com to lobby central government in order to establish the promotion of emotional literacy as a national priority with appropriate resources and a specific requirement for its inclusion in the National Curriculum.

Summary of Chapter 6: Emotional Literacy for local authorities

The heart of a strategy is a vision that young people will become adult citizens who are able to recognise, understand, handle, and appropriately express their emotions.

An emotionally literate school is one that recognises the value and importance of inclusion and spends time on seeking effective solutions to make it possible.

Developing an emotional literacy strategy—Steps to success:

Step 1: Establish a partnership between two or more senior officers.
Step 2: Begin with the individual so that the whole process is built on each of us exploring our own emotional literacy.
Step 3: Plan an awareness-raising programme of seminars, presentations and publications for head teachers, governors, parents, pupils, police, and others.
Step 4: Publish widely that emotional literacy is a primary priority, ranked on a par with literacy and numeracy and embed this prominently in the authority's Education Development Plan.
Step 5: Establish an Emotional Literacy Interest Group with a diverse range of people chosen from a wide variety of stakeholder groups.
Step 6: Demonstration or pilot projects should be undertaken in schools, the LEA, and in multi-agency settings.
Step 7: Evaluation of implementation of emotional literacy strategy should be planned in from the outset.
Step 8: Incorporate emotional literacy strategy in all major plans including the Education Development Plan, Behaviour Support Plan, Early Years Plan, Connexions, etc.

Michael Barber (2000), Head of the Standards and Effectiveness Unit, DfEE:
Teaching thinking skills in a disciplined way will have a positive effect on raising standards and related to the work on thinking skills is the development of strategies to enhance emotional literacy.

National Emotional Literacy Interest Group (NELIG) has been established:

http://www.nelig.com

Aims to become *the* resource for educators trying to promote emotional literacy.

Antidote: The Campaign for Emotional Literacy – James Park, Director

www.antidote.org.uk   *emotionalliteracy@antidote.org.uk*

Action

1. **Establish an emotional literacy interest group** in *your* local authority and recognise that this is a three-to-five year project at a minimum.
2. **Follow the Steps** outlined above or construct a programme bespoke to your individual needs.
3. **Encourage your local council and MPs** to support your emotional literacy initiative.
4. **Join Antidote** (individual or corporate membership).
5. **Contribute to nelig.com** and network with other friends of NELIG. Publish details of any projects you undertake and share vignettes of good practice.

Chapter 7

Emotional Literacy may be the hard option

All things are difficult before they are easy.

John Norley

The cult of the individual, in the western world, peaked during the 1980s and 1990s but the unrestrained drive to greater and greater excess has seen the emergence of a growing underclass. People perceive a wider divide between the 'haves' and the 'have nots', and the level of disaffection and dangerous disengagement in schools, communities, and the wider society is creating great tensions that sometimes end in that ultimate example of emotional illiteracy, the emotional hijacking that occurs when people are killed for the most trivial of reasons. One sentence set the ominous tone for many years to come: 'There is no such thing as society.' Western social policy then polarised further, with the sometimes explicit but more frequently implicit notion of the 'deserving poor' and the corollary... the 'undeserving poor'. One consequence of this zeitgeist has been that there is a universal desire to improve standards in schools, to promote growth in economies, and to increase the competitiveness of national economies. Now all of these might be possible and desirable if greater heed was also paid to ethics, sustainability, equality of opportunity and civilised safety nets for those who simply cannot cope.

The frequent inability of leading politicians and other major decision makers to recognise the importance of feelings and the appropriate expression and management of emotions is demonstrated daily, and often very publicly. Emotions, and hence emotional literacy, is sometimes derided or rejected as too 'touchy-feely' or as 'psychobabble', usually by people (and mostly men) who are at the lower end of the emotional literacy spectrum themselves. In contrast, those who have chosen genuinely to try and understand what it might mean and what benefits there may be for us all in trying to improve our own emotional literacy will be more circumspect in making hasty judgements about its worth.

The business world has recognised that promoting emotional literacy confers advantage to companies seeking competitive edge, and there is a speedily growing market of organisations offering the consultancy to make this a reality. Daniel Goleman (1998) asserts that: 'In professional and technical fields, the threshold for entry is typically top-quartile IQ of 110–120… Since everyone is in the top 10 per cent or so of intelligence, IQ itself offers relatively little competitive advantage.' Research on more than 500 organisations by the Hay Group and Goleman (1998) shows that:

- EQ (Emotional Quotient) accounts for over 85 per cent of outstanding performance in top leaders;
- EQ – not IQ – predicts top performance;
- EQ can be enhanced through specialised coaching development.

Chris Watkins (2000) notes that:

> Top managers can add or destroy huge economic value, and the higher the leverage – so the greater is the impact. Important are the 'hard' results such as improved profitability from higher productivity, increased sales and lowered costs, as well as 'softer' results from increased morale and motivation, greater cooperation, lower turnover and loss of talent.

Put simply, we need to develop 'hard' and 'soft' skills and use corresponding measures to estimate success.

I would assert that the case for promoting the emotional literacy of children and families is therefore even more crucial to future success, since the children of today are the leaders of tomorrow. Surely what we all want is to promote well-rounded citizens capable of making a real and positive contribution to society? If so, promoting emotional literacy is a natural option, but no one doubts how hard it may be in practice.

Emotional literacy for the individual

A theme throughout this book has been that of 'begin with yourself'; use reflection, and perhaps testing, to evaluate your own emotional literacy and then decide which areas of your EQ you would like to work on. Robert Cooper and Ayman Sawaf (1998) suggest that:

> It is through the voice of emotions – rather than thoughts alone – that we are prompted to:
>
> - Listen
> - Clarify
> - Value
> - Stand up and step forward
> - Learn and innovate
> - Consider
> - Remember
> - Empathize
> - Change and motivate

The term 'emotional literacy' was coined by Claude Steiner (1997) over twenty years ago, and the processes involved in its promotion are not new, simply restated and reframed in a contemporary idiom that recognises the pressing need for understanding their importance. Steiner suggests that as individuals we need to develop a new form of personal non-abusive power known as charisma. He then goes on to describe seven sources of non-abusive power, (rooted in Eastern religions), that may be summarised as:

1. *Balance:* the capacity to be rooted or grounded developed from knowing where you stand.
2. *Passion:* the power of passion can invigorate like nothing else... and this includes all forms of passion from the sexual to missionary zeal, to quixotic quests.
3. *Control:* especially important when, in the form of self-discipline, it lets you regulate other powers, such as passion, information, communication, and your emotions. Controlling emotions results in a powerful personal approach.
4. *Love:* which can be underdeveloped – leading to lack of warmth or empathy, or overdeveloped – leading to making excessive sacrifices for others while neglecting the self. What Steiner describes as a 'heart-centred approach to living' is characterised by; love of self, love of others and love of truth... the basis of honest communication.
5. *Communication:* two operations are involved: sending and receiving, speaking and listening... your link to others.
6. *Information:* is the antidote to uncertainty and Steiner describes information as coming in four forms; science (facts), intuition ('educated guesses'), wisdom (historical perspective), and vision (ability to see what lies ahead).
7. *Transcendence:* rising above it all, realising how insignificant we are in the universe, allowing us to get beyond our immediate concerns.

Steiner talks about using emotional literacy training as a tool for social change by people who apply it in their personal lives, and he calls such people 'Emotional Warriors'. So as an emotional warrior you are an individual who needs:

- balance to stand your ground;
- passion to energise you;
- control to keep a steady course;
- communication to interact effectively with others;
- information to make accurate predictions;
- transcendence to keep perspective;
- love to harmonise and give all these capacities a powerful forward thrust.

If we accept the challenge that promoting our own emotional literacy makes us fit for the purpose of helping others to promote their emotional literacy, then the really hard choice is about whether or not we commit to action... to work on our self.

A group is just a collection of individuals, while a team is a group of

Emotional literacy for the group

people with a common purpose. An organisation is made up of a number of groups of people, but a successful organisation is made up of teams. Earlier in this book we discussed the importance of explicit goals with tangible outcome measures, and successful organisations achieve that success by 'sticking to the knitting' or staying focused on the goals, objectives, and the component processes needed to meet these. Few organisations stay successful for long periods, and usually the reason for the downturn is a failure to adapt to changing circumstances. It could be argued that schools are at such a turning point, as advanced by Dalin (1995), and the number of 'beacon' schools is far smaller than the number of schools with 'serious weaknesses' or in 'special measures' to use current OFSTED-speak.

How successfully a school functions is dependent on a number of factors, but team communication is easily one of the most important. Weisenger (1998) describes how team success is directly related to effective communication in group situations, and cites the difference between meetings that are magical, have electric energy as people share/revise/support/come up with creative solutions and leave the meeting feeling terrific. In contrast we've all endured meetings where one person dominates, ruthlessly trounces other's ideas, discussions go in circles and everyone leaves feeling frustrated and isolated. Weisenger suggests that we foster team communication by:

- *Using and encouraging self-disclosure:* share thoughts and feelings, rather than hide behind the shield of rationalisation when really the feelings may be more important – as when reorganisations are in the offing.
- *Practice and encourage dynamic listening:* use restatement, reality checking and build on replies – such as when territory or function may be shifting.
- *Engage in problem-solving:* use solution-focused thinking, even when the problem seems insurmountable – as for example if OFSTED have just given very bad news.
- *Use assertiveness and criticism necessary:* perpetual agreement is stifling, and an emotionally literate team is one that welcomes robust debate and constructive criticism – only your friend will tell you when you have egg on your face!

Weisenger also gives tips for implementing the above and these are intended to facilitate effective communication irrespective of your role in the team:

1. Be inclusive – try to talk to everyone.
2. Discourage dominance – by encouraging wider participation.
3. Be supportive – give positive recognition even when disagreeing.
4. Keep the emotional tenor at a manageable level – this means judging the climate that the team can cope with, mature teams cope with stronger challenges.
5. Invite disagreement – but make it responsible and humane.

6. Be aware of how each member participates and responds – step in to rescue people who are struggling.

Just as an individual has a range of emotional skills and competencies so too does a team, so organisations can be emotionally literate or emotionally illiterate. Higgs and Dulewicz (1999) suggest that a way to develop a picture of what an emotionally intelligent organisation might be like is to identify the organisation level equivalents of the seven components of emotional intelligence, as follows:

Self-awareness

The organisation is characterised by openness and sharing about how it feels about its purpose, clients, products or services, and stakeholders. This awareness extends to knowing how others perceive them.

Emotional resilience

The organisation can withstand and absorb criticism and attack, and manage these effectively, such that they do not detract from the common purpose.

Motivation

The goals are explicit, and distractions or difficulties do not divert from the long-term strategy. Short-term solutions are used rarely and only to help return to the long-term strategy.

Interpersonal Sensitivity

Processes are established which enable feelings, needs and motivations to be understood and used to inform strategies, actions and decisions.

Influence

The organisation is always able to present persuasive arguments to support the vision, values, and business strategy.

Decisiveness

Decision-making processes are well established but do not preclude rapid decisions being made on the basis of incomplete or ambiguous information, so the organisation can act intuitively.

Conscientiousness and integrity

The organisation can 'walk the talk', and 'talk the walk'. This means the organisation says what it means, means what it says, and does it. So there is congruence between the public and private persona of the organisation, and a defensible ethical stance at the core of the way business is done.

Higgs and Dulewicz assert that it is possible to measure the emotional intelligence of organisations using this framework, and go on to describe how some organisations are universally high on all components e.g. Virgin. Obviously, like individuals, organisations may be strong on some components and weaker on others, or indeed may do badly on all. Predictably, an organisation with no strengths in the components of emotional intelligence is at high risk of failure. Higgs and Dulewicz then go on to look at the interaction between the emotional intelligence of the individual and the organisation that they summarise as:

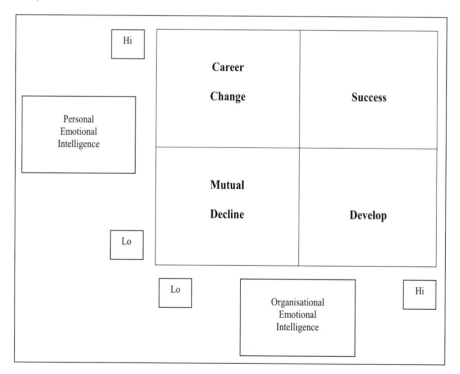

Table 7.1 Emotional Intelligence: Personal/Organisational Fit (Higgs and Dulewicz 1999)

We need to engage in a meaningful dialogue about precisely what we want our education system to deliver for the next 10–20 years. There are sterile and fatuous debates about who is responsible for raising standards, and particularly among individuals seeking to take the credit for any recent improvements. Clearly there can only be significant continuous improvement if all stakeholders are seeking to improve, so that includes learners, parents, teachers, other school staff, governors, support services, inspectors, and other agencies.

It is likely that the quality of teaching and learning has the greatest impact on standards, and so it is teachers who may be credited with the bulk of the effort involved in levering up standards of attainment (predominantly measured in narrow terms by Standard Assessment Tasks, Levels of Attainment in the National Curriculum, GCSEs and A levels). Furthermore, more and more schools are becoming sophisticated and mature in the way they use supported self-evaluation (with external critical friends including local inspectors or private consultants), such that the role of OFSTED also needs to change. OFSTED inspections are currently carried out based on a model that many experience as over-punitive and disabling, so a systematic and rigorous review of methodology is called for to see if there really is any justification for using the current model or whether standards could improve using more collaborative and emotionally literate practices.

Given the arguments set out above that EQ is more important than IQ in predicting future success, at least for those of average or above average IQ, then it is also time for a reappraisal of the best outcome measures for the educative process. An emotionally literate education system is one that considers holistic development of both the learners and the educators, in contrast to the slavish devotion to simplistic linear attainment test measures much beloved of politicians and the former chief inspector (HMCI). This is not an argument to do away with attainment testing, but to recognise its limitations and to look more closely at overall development. We need to establish an education system that produces young adults able to take their place in the world of work, to form and sustain enduring positive relationships, and to have regard to their role and place in the wider community.

To make this real and ground these views in observable good practice let us return to the work in progress in Southampton to promote emotional literacy and to further raise standards. From its inception, Southampton City Council Education Services set out to test the hypothesis that promoting emotional literacy will result in improved standards. As outlined earlier, this work includes the use of independent evaluation, and for Phase one of our initiative this has been undertaken by Professor Edmund Sonuga-Barke and Dr Robert Stratford from the University of Southampton, and generously funded independently by a grant from the Calouste

Emotional literacy for education

Gulbenkian Foundation. Sonuga-Barke and Stratford (2000) produced their report from which the following extracts are taken:

Emotional Literacy (EL) has been given the highest possible profile by the Education Service in Southampton. It is identified as a priority in Southampton City Council's Strategic Education Plan, and also in the School Improvement Plan. Defined as the ability to recognise, handle and appropriately express emotions, in both staff and pupils, it is held as being at the heart of the curriculum. It follows that improved levels of Emotional Literacy should be accompanied by improved standards and raised achievement in the more formal aspects of education. The city's initiative accords very well with government expectations that LEAs will take a lead in promoting social inclusion and citizenship, and with the recently commissioned Hay McBer report on effective teaching. It is also consistent with increasing national acceptance of the need to address behaviour problems from a primary prevention, whole school stance.

Considerable pioneering work by Southampton Psychology Service, together with an impetus from the city's curriculum policy and the work of Southampton's Inspectors, led to the formation of the Southampton Emotional Literacy Interest Group (SELIG). This group, with representatives from schools, governors, inspectors and other agencies, was instrumental in promoting EL projects on behalf of the City Council, and now meets regularly to monitor these activities.

The SELIG initiative was introduced during 1997–8, and contributing schools were invited to bid for financial support to start Emotional Literacy projects during 1999–2000. 12 projects received support in this way: 10 schools, a multi-agency provision and the Education Service itself. Funding was sought from the Gulbenkian Foundation to mount an external evaluation of the whole enterprise, and consultants were employed for this purpose in December 1999. The brief given for this work was to include formative feedback on each site's evaluation proposals, three site visits to review progress against the identified aims with key personnel, and a final report.

In the event, and in part as a consequence of the very ambitious programme set for introducing EL in Southampton, the evaluation process has not yet been completed. A total of 27 site visits was made by the consultants to the 11 projects actually started; three of the projects are still in process, and a further one discontinued. Final data or reports from internal evaluations were therefore anticipated from 7 sites (two of them joint) by the end of the 1999–2000 school year.

Have projects demonstrated change in EL?
As described above there are indications from all sites that the intervention has had an effect on components of EL. The 'quality' of the evidence for this varies from site to site and the extent to which EL has permeated the school culture also varies. In some settings the concept and enthusiasm seemed confined to the coordinator and

was not shared or known about by other staff; in other sites a clear whole school stance had been taken with EL as a major component of curriculum work across ages, and even across clusters. Future evaluation might well include baseline and post intervention readings of the level of penetration of the EL concept within a school staff.

Have projects demonstrated an improvement in standards?

The small scale and limited scope of the evaluations carried out to date mean that sites were not in a position to provide evidence at this stage of the effects of EL interventions on standards. This is as it should be at this stage. One would not expect the knock-on effects associated with the sorts of interventions carried out under the SELIG initiative to be manifest for some time. Such changes in standards are expected to follow only after the longer-term transformation of the whole school emotional culture. In one site it was made explicit that it might take a generation for a real shift in the emotional culture to have an impact across the catchment area – for instance in persuading parents to take a positive view of their children's educational performance (and limitations), and accept that their school was achieving the highest standards it could at that time.

Have the projects achieved the city's overall aims for EL?

The consultants felt that the SELIG initiative has had a positive general impact on the participating sites in the following ways:

(i)   an improved understanding of the nature of evidence based practice

(ii)   the development of research skills within each of the participating sites

(iii)   the empowerment of the coordinators and sites through a validatory dialogue with the external consultants

(iv)   the development of the construct of EL and its endorsement within sites through the involvement of staff, parents and children

(v)   the raising of awareness of EL within the formal curriculum of the participating schools

(vi)   the establishment of a supportive network through the SELIG group and the sharing of best practice across this group.

Clearly then there is still a lot to do as we move into Phase two of the emotional literacy strategy in Southampton, but there is also sufficient encouragement in the evaluation report to affirm the view that this work has legitimacy in and beyond Southampton. The principles from the project being carried out in Education Services (for details see Emotionally literate LEAs in Appendix 5) could serve as a model to any team or organisation seeking to operationalise emotional literacy within their organisation. We took the view that LEAs can only expect to facilitate the promotion of emotional literacy for children, families and school staff in Southampton if they look at promoting their own emotional literacy. Sonuga-Barke and Stratford describe the impact of this project as follows:

> In a first phase, all members of the Education Managers' Conference (22 people) had completed an Emotional Literacy (EL) assessment, involving a measure of Emotional Intelligence. 12 of these have so far received feedback on which to base learning action plans, to be reviewed later, and 4 have taken part in a 360-degree appraisal to include ratings of EL by their colleagues.
>
> At the end of the first phase, the project promised to have a very large impact, though this was likely to be at the level of raised awareness concerning the concept of EL among senior managers. Plans have now been made to shift the focus of the EL intervention from individual managers to the organisation (the Education Service), embedding the concepts of EL in the management process. This is to be achieved by the setting up of a Learning Hub: To assist managers in applying EL principles and practices to themselves and to others in their team. Objectives will include 'Staying effective under pressure', and 'Creating trust and building EL teams'. The coordination of this phase, to start in Summer 2001, will be handled by external personnel from the Centre for Applied Emotional Intelligence. This should help the service overcome a major obstacle to implementation of EL practice: the increased pressure of adopting and monitoring new approaches in an overworking culture.

I would argue that this activity could usefully be replicated in schools, the DfEE, OFSTED, and other agencies responsible for education. Undertaking such work is itself an indication of the emotional maturity of an organisation, since there are genuine risks attached to having your emotional literacy measured, and then trying to work on that in order to become more effective and efficient at work, but in a human and sustainable way.

By way of encouragement to other decision makers, movers and shakers within education to begin or continue this work to build a better education service, I'll conclude this section with a final extract from the Sonuga-Barke and Stratford report:

Major issues raised for the schools by participation in the project:

- The importance of EL as a contributory factor in raising standards was confirmed for many sites. The view that the academic improvements required couldn't be achieved without addressing other aspects of the 'whole' child appeared to be strengthened by involvement in the project.

- The need to extend the EL concept to parents, teachers and other staff within schools. It was deemed essential that EL permeated the whole ethos of a school, and reached all staff, if interventions were to be effective.

- The need to consider further adequate resourcing of the EL component of schoolwork – perhaps by funding coordinators with a specific brief for EL activity. The question of back-up may also need to be resolved given the problems occasioned by absence of the coordinator in some projects, leading to discontinuity.

- The need to ensure the consistent delivery of the EL initiative by all staff irrespective of their ideological point of view given that in some sites different teachers held more or less positive attitudes to the EL concept.

- The need to recognise that not all teachers have accepted the concept of EL yet and may need more preparation before full EL practice will be established.

- The importance of disseminating good practice from school to school, and the potential value of concerted action between schools.

- Overall the need for more evidence to persuade staff as to the benefits of EL interventions.

- The value of external facilitators was noted by the sites, but their involvement would need to start early in the life of projects to ensure adequate evaluation.

The consultants felt the Southampton Emotional Literacy Interest Group initiative has had a generally positive impact on the sites through a raised awareness of emotional literacy as an integral part of the formal curriculum, and an improved understanding of the nature of evidence based practice.

Emotional literacy for society

Throughout this book there has been an underlying message that nurturing emotional literacy begins with the self, and that through individual development comes collective and societal change for the better.

Without doubt there will be resistance to nurturing emotional literacy, especially from individuals who believe that most people are only interested in personal gain. Already there is a backlash from ill-informed pundits who try to belittle this ambitious agenda by writing it off as 'psychobabble', or 'liberal elitism'. At least if they consider the business case for nurturing emotional literacy then even this group will see that there is a hard-edged rationale for taking it more seriously, even if only to promote competitive edge.

My experience of presentation (each with written evaluation and feedback), consultancy and dialogue with over 4,000 educators in the last three years suggests that 'nurturing emotional literacy' strikes a chord with most, and nearly all recognise its potential importance.

The potential benefits to having a more emotionally literate society include:

- individuals who feel more valued, grounded, and connected to society;
- increased opportunity for individuals to contribute more to their own and other people's development;
- increased tolerance and even valuing of difference;
- more satisfying and enduring relationships;
- improved communication at home, at play and at work;
- improved mental, and so physical, health;
- improved desire to learn, and hence standards of learning (for all ages);
- greater recognition of everyone's uniqueness and that each person has value;
- greater recognition that conspicuous consumption is no real substitute for balancing all the areas of life: emotional literacy, physical health, work, family, friends, spiritual life, financial, recreational and leisure area of life;
- sustainable and ethical prosperity;
- improved ability to deal effectively and humanely with conflict;
- a genuinely inclusive society that is more pluralist in its orientation;
- humane and effective criminal justice system;
- greater participation in the democratic process, so improved ownership of the political agenda;
- leadership characterised by genuine involvement with the led, and leaders who also know how to follow.

The construction of an index of societal emotional literacy is entirely possible, and then government policy could be further tailored to secure improvement in each of the component constructs. In practice we could initially measure how emotionally literate a society is by considering a variety of indicators some of which are listed in Table 7.2. Careful interpretation of data would be required, as some of the characteristics listed have an indirect relationship to emotional literacy, however, these would offer a composite picture of how a society was functioning as shown in Table 7.2.

Indicator of societal EL	Indicator of societal EL	Indicator of societal EL
Number of homeless people	Number of crimes reported involving property	Levels of attainment at school
Number of people with non-organic mental illness Suicide rates	Number of murders and violent crimes reported	Reduced or no exclusions from school
	Number of unreported crimes (petty and serious)	Numbers of young people engaging in study beyond compulsory schooling
Self-harm and eating disorder rates	Rates of re-offending or recidivism following conviction or imprisonment	Numbers of people engaging in lifelong learning
Amount of reported and unreported racist attacks	Levels of child abuse	Proportion of graduates and postgraduates in the population
Amount of graffiti	Crimes against women (assault, rape, harassment)	Attendance rates and Truancy rates (including lessons)
Proportion of marriages ending in divorce	Employment and other economic indicators	Environmental indices e.g. carbon dioxide emission rates, % of waste that is recycled
Numbers of children with two biological parents living together	Maternity, paternity and carers leave arrangements, plus workplace crèche facilities	
Access to buildings (disability)	Employment rates for disabled	Minimum wage rates (and wage differentials)

Table 7.2 Indicators and proxy indicators of societal Emotional Literacy (Sharp 2001)

101

Each aspect of our lives potentially includes emotional literacy, whether in the context of education, health, economy, work, government, the criminal justice system or simply leisure. Our aim should be to secure a more holistic approach to each of these and to seek to make it possible for our self and others to have the opportunity to grow and develop well. We also need to elevate the quality of debate and dialogue in order to secure our aim.

Consider a recent education debate: Politicians argue in an immature and parochial way that is intended to polarise thinking in order to (over-)simplify the issues, and so try to win the hearts and minds of voters most often by appealing to base or selfish motives. For example in the *Times Educational Supplement* (TES 29 December 2000 New Year Debate) Tory Theresa May (Shadow Education Secretary) argues that there is a new liberal elite in education who believe they know what is best for children and are unwilling to trust the judgement of teachers. This liberal elite believes social deprivation is an excuse for poor levels of achievement, rather than recognising that education is the best way out for young people in such circumstances.

Predictably the contrary view is set out by Matthew Taylor (former assistant general secretary of the Labour Party) who argues that: 'If we can blame liberalism (for six-fold rise in exclusions in ten years), it is the economic neo-liberalism of monetarism and quasi-markets, not the progressive variety.' I suspect that both would subscribe to the belief that we should aim to provide a high-quality, well-rounded education that enables all to achieve their full potential, but the argument is deliberately couched in political terms and intentionally seeks to make much of points of disagreement rather than agreement.

Surely a more emotionally literate society is one that seeks to identify the key principles that most of us want to live by, and then seeks to find opportunities to make these the foundation of government policy irrespective of party political allegiance? Nurturing emotional literacy involves finding points of agreement and building on these, while at the same time promoting civilised and constructive disagreement where contrary or contrasting views are explored through genuine dialogue.

Our best hope of living in a more emotionally literate society is to seek to recognise, understand, handle, and appropriately express our own emotions. Then as parents, friends, educators or colleagues to demonstrate how that can help others to achieve their full potential.

Together we really could make a difference.

Shall we?

Summary of Chapter 7: Emotional Literacy may be the hard option

Raising standards, promoting growth and increasing competitiveness of national economies can be emotionally literate and desirable if heed is paid to ethics, sustainability, equality of opportunity and civilised safety nets for those who cannot cope.

Hay Group and Goleman (1998) show that:

- EQ (Emotional Quotient) accounts for over 85% of outstanding performance in top leaders;
- EQ – not IQ – predicts top performance;
- EQ can be enhanced through specialised coaching development.

'Emotional warrior' (Steiner 1997) is an individual who needs:

- Balance to stand your ground
- Passion to energise you
- Control to keep a steady course
- Communication to effectively interact with others
- Information to make accurate predictions
- Transcendence to keep perspective
- Love to harmonise and give all these capacities a powerful forward thrust.

Weisinger (1998): **Tips for emotionally literate teamwork:**

1. Be inclusive
2. Discourage dominance
3. Be supportive
4. Keep the emotional tenor at a manageable level
5. Invite disagreement
6. Be aware of how each member participates and responds

Engage in a meaningful dialogue about precisely what we want our education system to deliver for the next 10–20 years.

An emotionally literate education system is one that considers holistic development of both the learners and the educators.

'Southampton's initiative has had a generally positive impact through a raised awareness of emotional literacy as an integral part of the formal curriculum, and an improved understanding of the nature of evidence based practice.'

Nurturing emotional literacy begins with the self, and through individual development comes collective and societal change for the better.

An emotionally literate society is one that seeks to identify the key principles that most of us want to live by, and then seeks to find opportunities to make these the foundation of government policy irrespective of party political allegiance.

Action

Plan to assess your own emotional literacy either through the activities in this book or more formally by having a psychometric assessment (preferably 360 degree, involving input from colleagues in giving their view of your emotional literacy).

Develop a personal action plan and share with a learning partner (a trusted friend or colleague). Which characteristics of an emotional warrior would you like to further develop?

In your work team get each member to rate the team emotional literacy on the headings (use 1=low 10 = high):

- Self-awareness
- Emotional reliance
- Motivation
- Interpersonal sensitivity
- Decisiveness
- Influence
- Conscientiousness and integrity.

Draft an action plan to promote team emotional literacy, and have this as a standing item on team meetings for monitoring.

Form an Emotional Literacy Interest Group in your LEA or School and use the structures and procedures outlined above to begin to develop a 3- to 5-year plan (Buddy-up with another LEA or School to act as a learning partner and to share ideas).

Lobby your local councillors or MP or MEP to make emotional literacy an issue at their next election. How can you contribute to building a more emotionally literate society?

Appendices

These pages may be photocopied for use within the purchasing institution. Otherwise, all rights are reserved.

1. Taking Stock (blank pro-forma)
2. My Journey Along Life's Highway (blank pro-forma)
3. Emotionally literate families
4. Emotionally literate schools
5. Emotionally literate LEAs
6. Emotionally literate organisations
7. Emotion – a vocabulary
8. Emotional Literacy: Activities for 4- to 11-year-olds *
9. Emotional Literacy: Activities for 11- to 16-year-olds *
10. Emotional Literacy: Diary of feelings

* See also:
 50 Activities for Teaching: Emotional Intelligence (1996)
 The Best From Innerchoice Publishing, PO Box 1185,
 Torrance, California 90505

Taking Stock

Development area:	Rating on ___ (date)	Priority for change High/Med/Low	What I will do to change things:	Review date:
1. Emotional Literacy				
2. Physical Health				
3. Work				
4. Family and/or Partner				
5. Friends				
6. Spiritual				
7. Financial				
8. Recreation, Hobbies, Holidays				

My Journey Along Life's Highway

Guidelines for completing 'My Journey Along Life's Highway'

1. Start from when you were born, at the bottom of the sheet and continue up to present day or beyond to your chosen future.
2. Put in all the milestones and events that you feel have been important in your life.
3. Include any achievements that you're pleased about, and some less happy experiences that have influenced you.
4. You can use words, images, dates, or symbols that help to tell the story of your journey so far.
5. On the back of the sheet:
   - (a) Write a list of things you feel good about in your life
   - (b) Can you say why you do the job you do?
   - (c) How might you answer the question: 'What is the most important thing life has taught me?'
6. If you feel it is appropriate, then share your work with someone.
7. In what ways can you help to nurture
   - (a) your emotional literacy
   - (b) children's emotional literacy?

If this activity evokes painful memories then talk to a trusted friend or partner. If its impact is overwhelming then seek an appointment to discuss it with your GP or a qualified psychologist or psychotherapist.

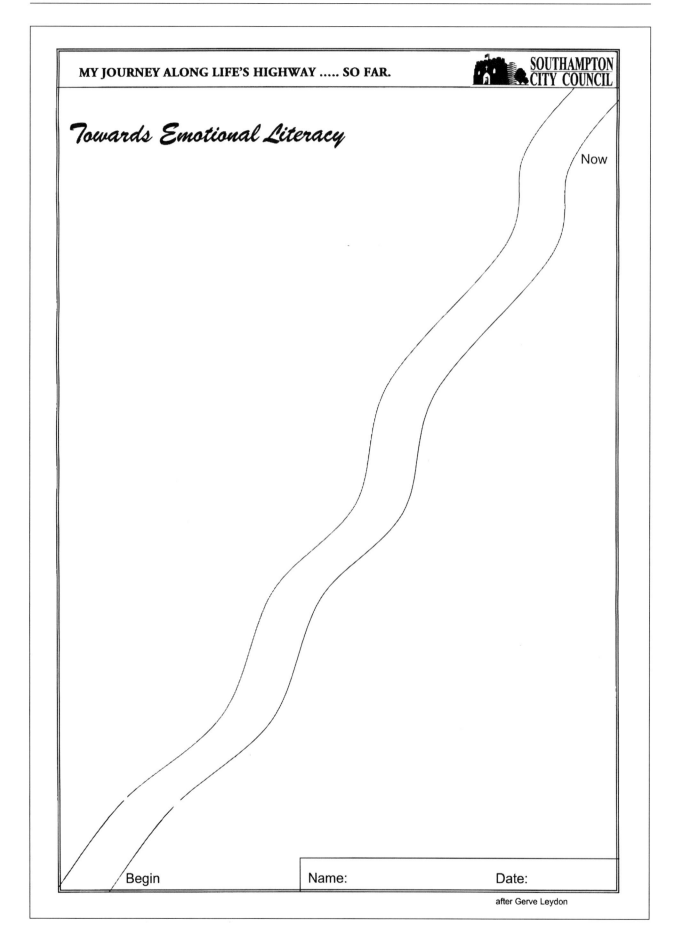

MY JOURNEY ALONG LIFE'S HIGHWAY ..... SO FAR.

SOUTHAMPTON
CITY COUNCIL

Towards Emotional Literacy

Now

Begin

Name:

Date:

after Gerve Leydon

Emotionally literate families

Give your rating on each of the scales below where 1 = very low and 10 = very high, for how you think your family scores then discuss what you would like to *keep the same or change:*

1. The family communication is open, honest, and mostly civilised

    1   2   3   4   5   6   7   8   9   10

2. Parent(s) is/are happy to show affection to their children

    1   2   3   4   5   6   7   8   9   10

3. Parent(s) is/are usually calm, controlled and considerate towards children

    1   2   3   4   5   6   7   8   9   10

4. Parent(s) recognise that they make mistakes, and are relaxed about saying sorry

    1   2   3   4   5   6   7   8   9   10

5. The family sits together regularly to eat meals and value this time

    1   2   3   4   5   6   7   8   9   10

6. Children are able to discuss difficult or distressing issues with their parent(s)

    1   2   3   4   5   6   7   8   9   10

7. The family go on outings or trips together and make time for shared activities

    1   2   3   4   5   6   7   8   9   10

8. The family members feel safe and secure together

    1   2   3   4   5   6   7   8   9   10

9. There are more affirmations and positive comments than hostile criticisms

    1   2   3   4   5   6   7   8   9   10

10. Family members have genuine empathy for each other's difficulties

    1   2   3   4   5   6   7   8   9   10

11. Family members have high expectations of success for each other

    1   2   3   4   5   6   7   8   9   10

Emotionally literate schools

Give your rating on each of the scales below where 1 = very low and 10 = very high, for how you think your school scores then draw up a simple but realistic improvement plan:

1. The school is generally child-centred and the children would agree with that view

   1   2   3   4   5   6   7   8   9   10

2. The school is generally parent friendly and welcomes them as members of the school community

   1   2   3   4   5   6   7   8   9   10

3. The school is calm and orderly most of the time

   1   2   3   4   5   6   7   8   9   10

4. Behaviour in the school is generally good, both pupils and staff feel safe and secure

   1   2   3   4   5   6   7   8   9   10

5. There is an explicit and shared understanding of what emotional literacy means by staff

   1   2   3   4   5   6   7   8   9   10

6. There is an explicit and shared understanding of what emotional literacy means by parents

   1   2   3   4   5   6   7   8   9   10

7. There is an explicit and shared understanding of what emotional literacy means by governors

   1   2   3   4   5   6   7   8   9   10

8. There is clear evidence that emotional literacy is routinely included beyond the taught curriculum

   1   2   3   4   5   6   7   8   9   10

9. The staff and governor training agenda includes emotional literacy and each has a named person with lead responsibility for monitoring and evaluating how emotional literacy is being promoted

   1   2   3   4   5   6   7   8   9   10

10. The school has a clear policy on how it promotes inclusion and contingencies for dealing with even the most challenging youngsters

   1   2   3   4   5   6   7   8   9   10

11. There is a supportive and encouraging management team who motivate staff well

    1   2   3   4   5   6   7   8   9   10

12. The staff room is a welcoming and pleasant area that people actually enjoy using, and visitors are also welcomed

    1   2   3   4   5   6   7   8   9   10

13. There is clear evidence of good communication between staff, staff and pupils, staff and parents

    1   2   3   4   5   6   7   8   9   10

14. The school displays are high quality, imaginative, changed regularly and attractive to look at

    1   2   3   4   5   6   7   8   9   10

15. There is an active and well-regarded school council (or similar structure) that gives children a real say in influencing the life of the school

    1   2   3   4   5   6   7   8   9   10

16. Staff can expect help without fear of ridicule or negativity if they are having difficulties of any sort, with clear evidence of empathic support

    1   2   3   4   5   6   7   8   9   10

17. Decision-making is usually participative and staff feel they have a real say in how things happen

    1   2   3   4   5   6   7   8   9   10

18. Generally staff feel positive about their work, albeit that it is often very challenging

    1   2   3   4   5   6   7   8   9   10

19. There is a named emotional literacy coordinator who is a member of senior management

    1   2   3   4   5   6   7   8   9   10

20. Overall staff feel optimistic that they are making a positive difference for children

    1   2   3   4   5   6   7   8   9   10

Emotionally literate LEAs

5.1 The project plan for Southampton

1.
School/Agency:	*SOUTHAMPTON LEA, EDUCATION SERVICES*
Address:	*Peter Sharp, Principal Educational Psychologist,*
	Frobisher House, Nelson Gate, Southampton SO15 1BZ

   Phone: 02380–833106   Fax: 02380–833033   e-mail: p.sharp@southampton.gov.uk

2.
   Project Statement

   We aim to assess the emotional literacy of education services and then plan how to promote our emotional literacy in order to be more efficient and effective.

3.
   Project Director: *Peter Sharp*
   Post (eg. Head / Dep H/T / PEP): *PEP*
   Contact phone: *02380–833106*   e-mail: p.sharp@southampton.gov.uk

4.
   Project Objectives

   1. *To comprehensively assess the emotional literacy of each section within education services and then collate this in order to establish development priorities.*
   2. *At the end of the first phase of the project (Summer 2000) we will have a clear plan for promoting our emotional literacy in order to become more efficient and effective.*
   3. *Managers will be expected to incorporate this work into section plans with measurable outcomes and all activities fully costed (e.g. cost of assessment, preparation and delivery of training, monitoring and evaluation).*
   4. *Stakeholders beyond education services (e.g. head teachers, parents, and children) will be actively encouraged to support and contribute to this project.*

5. Work undertaken to promote a shared understanding of Emotional Literacy:
Definition:
> *Seminars, presentations, and development events held to raise awareness of emotional literacy including the Southampton definition. E.g. Education Managers Conference, all EPs and Inspectors, SELIG, newsletters, committee report. Inclusion of Emotional Literacy in: Strategic Education Plan, School Improvement Plan, Behaviour Support Plan, Early Years Plan.*

How objectives are to be achieved:

- *Train assessors in EQ (PEP + SEP).*
- *Assess EQ of Education Managers.*
- *Assess Emotional Literacy of sections/teams (partly as systems or institutions and partly as a collection of individuals).*
- *Hold further seminars and briefings to coordinate planning and benchmark sections/teams re EL*
- *Publish a training agenda and link up with Investors In People and Quality Assurance mechanisms.*
- *Cost the implementation of the plan and secure funding (could be existing fund and/ or new money).*
- *Monitor and evaluate implementation.*

How project contributes to wider EL aims:
> *Education Services can only expect to facilitate the promotion of Emotional Literacy for children, families, and school staff in Southampton if they look at promoting their own emotional literacy. Our aim is to test the hypothesis that*
> *IMPROVING EMOTIONAL LITERACY = IMPROVING STANDARDS*
> *and our belief that*
> *EMOTIONAL LITERACY IMPROVES AND INCREASES YOUR LIFE CHANCES.*

6. What benchmarks have you got before project started?
Hard data: (Quantitative) *Efficiency and effectiveness data from Education Services Performance Review in 1999, and later in Spring/Summer 2000, gives section by section analysis. Currently no quantitative data on EQ or EL for sections or services: essentially benchmark will be Year 2000 data and compare again in 2001.*
Soft data: (Qualitative) *Considerable evidence of significant overworking (self-report and diary analysis) across education services, feedback in appraisal showing that current working practices are not sustainable in the long term.*

7. What improvements are you hoping to see

- Directly: *Improvements in emotional literacy of individuals, teams and education services. These benchmarked against individual, team and service assessments. As EL improves we expect some improvement in efficiency and effectiveness and a greater practical acceptance of over-capacity issues should lead to more rational planning of 'the possible' rather than the 'hoped for'. Achieving Investors In People accreditation is one measure of EL in the system.*

> • Indirectly: *People should report feeling more positive about their work and recognise the benefit of obtaining a healthier balance in their lives (home/work/interests).*
> *The 'massive overworking' culture should dissipate in a sustainable way. Evidence of working smarter not harder should be explicit.*
>
> as a result of undertaking this work?

8. What have you done to link policies on

   • learning and achievement
   • behaviour and discipline
   • health promotion
   • PSHE
   • spiritual, moral and cultural development
   • equal opportunities
   • citizenship
   • social inclusion
   • crime and disorder?

   Our aim in all the work undertaken by Education Services in promoting EL is to encourage and support schools in making the links with their policies, and ensuring that LEA policies are compatible with this too. Activities to further this include:

9. How does your project help to 'establish emotional literacy at the heart of the curriculum'?
   The LEA is taking a lead role in critically examining its own emotional literacy in tandem with a host of project based activities and a citywide strategy to promote EL. The first phase of this work is being independently evaluated by consultants from Southampton University, which will inform our future planning: 2000–2005. It is anticipated that psychologists, inspectors and officers will work together to monitor, evaluate and foster the establishment of EL at the heart of the curriculum in the course of their routine visits to schools and through separately commissioned activity.

10. Where does this work fit in your development plan? (Quote extracts if applicable.)

    This work is well documented in:

    1. Strategic Education Plan; Key Issue 1
    2. Behaviour Support Plan 1998–2001
    3. School Improvement Plan 1998–2001
    4. Education Committee Report 1999
    5. Emotional Literacy Guidelines (Draft) for publication Summer 2000.

11. Can you produce evidence to show that promoting emotional literacy raises standards?
    The independent evaluation by consultants from Southampton University will be able to detect any 'green shoots' of improvement, but it is not expected that we can answer this

question with confidence until the end of 2001. Trend analysis may allow us to evaluate the relative contribution of promoting Emotional Literacy to the overall city aim of improving standards for all children in the city. Further work is planned to look at the percentage of variance accounted for by EL in the school improvement agenda.

12. Have you produced some examples of good practice to share with colleagues?
At the time of writing these are being collected. (January 2001)

13. How does this all fit in with the notion of continuous improvement – can we do better and feel better?
This initiative can only work if people genuinely believe that there are real benefits. This means benefits for children, families and for every individual working in Education Services. Our aim is to humanise the continuous improvement process, so that people feel encouraged and not overwhelmed by it.

14. What has not worked to promote emotional literacy? (e.g. Learning point from a project that has not worked as you hoped)
The pace of development of this initiative has been over-ambitious, and needed us to revise the timescale for completing the development of the guidelines, consultation and subsequent implementation. It is likely that a phased introduction is more tenable, so that 12 projects (10 schools) are in place 1999–2000 and then many schools will join the strategy in 2000–2001, with the remainder joining in 2001–2002.

PROMOTING EMOTIONAL LITERACY:

'People are able to recognise, understand, handle,
and appropriately express their emotions.'

Southampton aims to
'establish emotional literacy at the heart of the curriculum.'

5.2 The use of the Emotional Intelligence Questionnaire

SELIG 2000–2001
Developing the emotional literacy of Education Services
EMOTIONAL INTELLIGENCE QUESTIONNAIRE (EIQ)
Prof Victor Dulewicz and Dr Malcolm Higgs

Introduction

As part of Southampton's strategy to promote Emotional Literacy (EL) we are providing the opportunity for all education service managers to develop firstly their own, and later their team's, emotional literacy. In the first phase all managers will complete the emotional intelligence questionnaire (EIQ) and subsequently draw up a personal action plan having had the EIQ feedback.

In the second phase, service managers will assess the emotional literacy of their sections or teams and the individuals within them, and then go on to write and implement a team development plan for raising EL.

This work is part of a larger citywide strategy for promoting EL for staff and pupils in all our schools. Currently there are 11 schools carrying out pilot projects to promote EL and these, together with a multi-agency project and the education services project, are the subject of an independent evaluation being carried out by Southampton University and funded by the Calouste Gulbenkian Foundation.

Southampton defines emotional literacy as: *the ability to recognise, understand, handle, and appropriately express emotions.*

This definition is consistent with that of Daniel Goleman (1997):

- Knowing what you are feeling, and being able to handle those feelings without them swamping you;
- Being able to motivate yourself to get jobs done, to be creative, and to perform at your peak;
- Sensing what others are feeling, and handling relationships effectively.

The Emotional Intelligence Questionnaire (EIQ)

Goleman (1996) asserts that IQ at best contributes about 20 per cent of the factors that determine success in life. Dulewicz and Higgs (1999) assert that there is a relationship between emotional literacy and other competencies. Perhaps even more significant is their belief that emotional intelligence can be developed. For this reason Southampton has chosen to use the term emotional literacy rather than emotional intelligence, since it better reflects the ability of the individual to develop skills and competencies connected with EL.

So managers need to learn both cognitively based skills and competencies, and 'how to feel about what they do and learn'.

The EIQ is an instrument that has been developed and evaluated both in terms of reliability and validity, and has a high degree of correlation with other instruments including the Myers Briggs Personality Type Inventory, Cattell's 16PF, the OPQ and Competencies (JCS). The initial standardisation was completed on 196 managers undertaking an MBA at Henley Management College in 1998. Some descriptors of this sample include:

- Mean age 35.5
- Mean salary £51.2K
- Mean staff managed 77.4
- Mean levels to the CEO 2.2
- 76% male
- 80% private sector.

New norms are being developed for more general populations and for specific client groups (e.g. head teachers, army officers, etc.).

EIQ Scale descriptions

Scale A: Self-awareness

Ability to recognise and manage one's own feelings in a way that feels that one can control.
Above average score... tend to control and manage moods well and have a positive outlook.
Below average score... tend either to be unaware of feelings or to feel swamped by them.

Scale B: Emotional resilience

Ability to perform consistently in a range of situations under pressure and to adapt behaviour appropriately.
Above average score... tend to adjust readily to new situations and circumstances, and deliver performance commitments.
Below average score... tend to find performance suffers when faced with personal challenge and criticism.

Scale C: Motivation

The drive and energy to achieve clear results and make an impact, and to balance long- and short-term goals.
Above average score... tend to focus on the need to achieve results and complete the task.
Below average score... tend to prevaricate and avoid commitment to results and action.

Scale D: Interpersonal sensitivity

Facility to be aware of, and take account of, the needs and perceptions of others.
Above average score... tend to focus on explaining problems and issues and to accept that the solution of others may be more practical than their own preferred solution.
Below average score... tend to impose goals and solutions on others, rarely adapting their views in the face of others.

Scale E: Influence

Ability to persuade others to change a viewpoint based on the understanding of their position, and to provide a rationale for change.
Above average score... tend to be effective in winning others over.
Below average score... find it difficult to win the support of others for their ideas.

Scale F: Decisiveness

Ability to arrive at clear decisions and drive their implementation through, even with ambiguous or incomplete information to go on.
Above average score... and to make decisions even in difficult circumstances, and obtain support for these ideas.
Below average score... tend to seek certainties and are risk-aversive, low tolerance of ambiguity.

Scale G: Conscientiousness and integrity

Ability to display clear commitment to a course of action in the face of challenge, words and deeds match. Ethical solutions always sought.
Above average score... strong commitment to both agreed goals and methods of working, 'ends justify means' eschewed.
Below average score... willing to compromise personal or organisational values in order to achieve goals.

In addition to the above we are starting to use a 360-degree version of the EIQ which involves both self-report and colleague (peer/subordinate/superior) report, where scores are compared and a composite and more accurate picture of the individual's emotional intelligence is obtained.

References

Goleman, D. (1997) 'Beyond IQ: Developing the leadership competencies of emotional intelligence'. Paper presented at Second International Competency Conference London, October 1997.
Goleman, D. (1996) *Emotional Intelligence: Why it Can Matter More than IQ*. London: Bloomsbury.
Dulewicz, V. and Higgs, M. (1999) *Emotional Intelligence Questionnaire: User Guide*. Windsor: NFER-Nelson.

5.3 Action Plan following EIQ measurement

EDUCATION SERVICES PROMOTING EMOTIONAL LITERACY
CONFIDENTIAL
DEVELOPMENTAL ACTION PLAN

NAME _____

LEARNING PARTNER _____

DATE OF COMPLETION _____

DATE FOR FIRST REVIEW_____

DATE FOR SECOND REVIEW_____

To be completed after the administration of EIQ and following feedback session and discussion.

EIQ Scale	Development idea	First review	Second review
Scale 1: *Self-awareness*			
Scale 2: *Emotional resilience*			
Scale 3: *Motivation*			

EIQ Scale	Development idea	First review	Second review
Scale 4: *Interpersonal* *sensitivity*			
Scale 5: *Influence*			
Scale 6: *Decisiveness*			
Scale 7: *Conscientiousness* *and integrity*			

PLAN BEYOND THE SECOND REVIEW:

Give your rating on each of the scales below where 1 = very low and 10 = very high, for how you think your LEA scores then draw up a simple but realistic improvement plan:

1. There is clear evidence that the LEA listens to those it serves.

    1   2   3   4   5   6   7   8   9   10

2. Communication in the LEA is good and characterised by openness and honesty

    1   2   3   4   5   6   7   8   9   10

3. There is respect and understanding between members of the LEA for each other's roles

    1   2   3   4   5   6   7   8   9   10

4. Almost all staff takes responsibility for the organisation and not just their team or service

    1   2   3   4   5   6   7   8   9   10

5. The LEA recruitment and retention strategy includes emotional literacy as a factor.

    1   2   3   4   5   6   7   8   9   10

6. The LEA fosters a 'no blame' culture where calculated risk and innocent errors are understood

    1   2   3   4   5   6   7   8   9   10

7. The LEA tries to implement family friendly policies, including flexible working practices

    1   2   3   4   5   6   7   8   9   10

8. The LEA promotes sustainable working practices, and fosters personal and professional development

    1   2   3   4   5   6   7   8   9   10

9. The LEA actively measures and monitors emotional literacy of individuals and services

    1   2   3   4   5   6   7   8   9   10

10. The LEA investigates the link between emotional literacy and learning

    1   2   3   4   5   6   7   8   9   10

Emotionally literate organisations

Give your rating on each of the scales below where 1 = very low and 10 = very high, for how your organisation scores then draw up a simple but realistic improvement plan:

1. The organisation includes emotional literacy as part of its strategic development plan

    1   2   3   4   5   6   7   8   9   10

2. The organisation shows care for the health and welfare of all the staff

    1   2   3   4   5   6   7   8   9   10

3. Just as staff are expected to pursue continuous improvement, working conditions improve

    1   2   3   4   5   6   7   8   9   10

4. Values are explicit, shared and observed

    1   2   3   4   5   6   7   8   9   10

5. Knowledge, skills, and experience are more important than position, status or title

    1   2   3   4   5   6   7   8   9   10

6. The organisation seeks to involve all its members in decision-making

    1   2   3   4   5   6   7   8   9   10

7. The organisation recognises that good communication needs to be worked at

    1   2   3   4   5   6   7   8   9   10

8. Employee satisfaction is generally high

    1   2   3   4   5   6   7   8   9   10

9. People frequently give and receive praise and affirmation or recognition

    1   2   3   4   5   6   7   8   9   10

10. Employees are expected to lead a full and rich life outside work

    1   2   3   4   5   6   7   8   9   10

11. The organisation is high on implementing espoused values, beliefs, and principles

    1   2   3   4   5   6   7   8   9   10

Appendix 7

Emotion – a vocabulary

Emotion (a – c)	Emotion (d – f)	Emotion (f – j)	Emotion (l – r)	Emotion (s – z)
abandoned	deceitful	frustrated	languid	sad
abused	defeated	full	lazy	sapped
accepted	dejected	funky	left out	satisfied
adamant	delighted		lonely	sexy
acquiescent	dependent	glad	loser, like a	scared
adequate	depressed	good	lovable	screwed up
affectionate	deprived	grateful	loving	settled
affirmed	desperate	gratified	low	shallow
afraid	destructive	greedy	loyal	shocked
agonised	determined	grieving		shy
alarmed	different	groovy	manipulated	silly
alienated	diffident	guilty	mawkish	sluggish
ambivalent	diminished	gullible	miserable	sorry
annoyed	disappointed	gutless	misunderstood	spiritual
anxious	discontented	gutted		strained
apathetic	distracted		nasty	stunned
appreciated	distraught	happy	needy	stupid
astounded	disturbed	hateful	nervous	sure
attractive	divided	helpful	nice	
avaricious	dominated	helpless		tempted
averse	dubious	high	odd	tense
awed		homesick	opposed	threatened
awkward	eager	honoured	optimistic	thwarted
	ecstatic	hopeful	outraged	tired
bad	elated	hopeless	overlooked	torn
barmy	electrified	horny	overwhelmed	touched
balmy	embarrassed	horrible		touchy
beaten	empty	hostile	panicked	trapped
beautiful	enchanted	hurt	paranoid	truculent
betrayed	energetic	hysterical	peaceful	
bewildered	envious		persecuted	
bitter	evasive	ignored	petrified	unctuous
blissful	exasperated	immobilised	pleasant	upset
bold	excited	impatient	pleased	used
bored	exhausted	imposed upon	possessive	useless
brave	exhilarated	impressed	preoccupied	
burdened		inadequate	pressured	vacuous
butch	fabulous	incompetent	putrid	violent
	fantastic	infatuated		vivacious
callous	fawning	inferior	quarrelsome	vulnerable
caddish	fearful	infuriated	quiet	
cagey	flustered	inhibited		wilful
cantankerous	foolish	insecure	randy	wishy-washy
chided	frantic	insincere	refreshed	wonderful
churlish	free	inspired	rejected	worried
comfortable	fretful	intimidated	relaxed	
concerned	friendless	involved	relieved	zany
confident	friendly	isolated	remorseful	
cop-out	frightened		repulsive	
cowardly	frigid	jaded	restless	
creative		jealous	restrained	
curious		joyous		
cut off		judgemental		
		jumpy		

Emotional Literacy: Activities for 4- to 11-year-olds

Activity 1: Select a shorter list of words from the above list that are age or stage appropriate and then encourage children to:

(a) Mime that feeling and get others to guess it (so choose your list carefully!)
(b) Tell of a time when they have felt one of those emotions, say as part of circle time.
(c) Write a story or do a piece of creative writing that uses some of these words.
(d) Do a painting or drawing to depict that emotion and put up a 'feelings wall' or display in class or a corridor.

Activity 2: Ask the children to bring a treasured or valued object (e.g. toy, trinket, memento, photo, book, etc) and to describe what are the feelings they associate with the object. You need to have clear ground rules and have a good relationship with the group before embarking on this activity, and be able to protect and keep their objects safe and secure in school.

Activity 3: Children are asked to write a list of feelings words to describe what they like about a friend or relative (perhaps let them have a list of words from the above vocabulary). For children who cannot write simply have an oral lesson or you capture the information on the board.

Activity 4: Relaxation exercise – play some quiet mood music, dim the lights or use blackout if you have the option but keep some light. Get the children settled and comfy, ask them to notice how they are breathing, now breathe more slowly, in through your nose and out through your mouth but quietly, take deeper breaths, hold it for a few seconds… and exhale slowly. Encourage them to try this with eyes closed, and to notice the tension easing.

Emotional Literacy: Activities for 11- to 16-year-olds

Activity 1: Improving Self-awareness – ask the students to keep a feelings diary for a week (see Appendix 10) and then:

(a) Invite them to do a short account of how their mood or feeling changed from one session to another. Can they describe what influenced that change, was the feeling changed deliberately, was the change welcome?
(b) Ask students to describe the impact of their feeling(s) on other people, based on their experience described in the diary. E.g. If they felt happy did that help others to feel happier, conversely if they were cross did that seem to make others cross?

Activity 2: Handling difficult feelings – elicit some real examples of when people have felt happy, sad, angry, calm, exhausted, and energetic. Discuss, perhaps as a circle time activity, or through a drama workshop, or through writing, what they *felt, thought, and did*. Ask students to describe the nightmarish way to handle feelings (e.g. getting really angry back with someone who is angry, or being even more miserable than someone who is fed up), and the dream way to handle it. Be prepared to discuss how there is no clear-cut right or wrong way to handle feelings, but there are helpful and harmful ways.

Activity 3: Ask students to collect newspaper and magazine cuttings of articles and photos that show strong feelings, then make a group montage and put it on display. Use this to stimulate discussion about the way the media tend to portray feelings and emotions. Invite students to write the story very differently and avoiding sensationalism but maintaining some real human interest. Perhaps invite a journalist from your local paper to work with you on this activity.

Emotional Literacy: Diary of feelings

Simply write how you were feeling in each slot using words to sum up how each slot turned out. Use words, images (e.g. faces), rating scales (e.g. 1= miserable 10 = fantastic). At the end of the week complete the 'Reflection' column. Use the diary for a week or two and then decide what you would like to keep the same or change, there is more likelihood of change if you share your decision about what the change involves with a trusted friend or colleague. Maybe write a 'contract' with yourself and give it to a friend to post to you after one month to review how you're getting on.

Day	Morning	Afternoon	Evening	Reflection
Monday				
Tuesday				
Wednesday				
Thursday				
Friday				
Saturday				
Sunday				

References

Antidote, 5th Floor, 45 Beech Street, Barbican, London, EC2Y 8AD Tel. 020-7588-5151 e-mail: emotionalliteracy@antidote.org.uk

Apter, Terri (1997) *The Confident Child. Emotional Coaching for the Crucial Decade – Ages Five to Fifteen.* New York: W. W. Norton and Company Ltd.

Atkinson, R. L. *et al.* (2000) *Hilgard's Introduction to Psychology* (13th edn). New York: Harcourt Brace Jovanovich.

Ax, A. F. (1953) 'The Physiological differentiation of fear and anger in humans', Psychosomatic Medicine **15**, 422–433.

Barber, Michael (2000) 'Thinking for Learning' in *Managing Schools Today*. May 2000. Birmingham: Questions Publishing.

Bettelheim, Bruno (1988) *A Good Enough Parent*, London: Pan Books.

Bocchino, Rob (1999) *Emotional Literacy: To Be A Different Kind of Smart*. California: Sage Publications Company.

Borba, Michelle (1995) *Esteem Builders' Complete Program*. Torrance, California: Jalman Press.

Bowlby, John (1987) in Ann Shearer's 'Society Today', *The Guardian*, 22 July 1987.

Bowlby, John (1979) *The Making and breaking of Affectional Bonds*.

Brazelton, T. *et al.* (2000) *The Irreducible Needs of Children: What Every Child Must Have to Grow, Learn and Flourish*. Merloyd Lawrence Book/Perseus Publishing.

Brighouse, Tim (2000) Unpublished presentation: 'How Some Schools Stretch Success to New Levels' at Service Children's Education Conference in Loccum, Germany (25 October).

Cannon, W. B. (1927) 'The James-Lange theory of emotions: A critical re-examination and an alternative theory', *American Journal of Psychology* **39**, 106–124.

Cherniss, Cary and Adler, Mitchel (2000) *Promoting Emotional Intelligence in Organisations*. Alexandria, VA: American Society for Training and Development (ASTD).

Clarke, Jean and Dawson, Connie (1998) *Growing Up Again: Parenting Ourselves, Parenting Our Children*. Minnesota: Hazelden.

Coleman, Paul (2000) *Smart Talk: The Six Ways We Speak to Our Kids*. New Jersey: Prentice Hall Press.

Cooper, R. and Sawaf, A. (1998) *Executive EQ: Emotional Intelligence in Leadership and Organisations*. New York, Perigree Business: The Berkley Publishing Group.

Coopersmith, S. (1967) *The Antecedents of Self-esteem*. San Francisco: Freeman.

Covey, Stephen R. (1989 reissued 1999) *The 7 Habits of Highly Effective People*. London: Simon and Schuster.

Dalin, Per with Rolff, H. G. (1995) *Changing the School Culture*. London: Cassell.

Darwin, Charles (1872) *The Expression of Emotions in Man and Animals*. N.Y. Philosophical Library, 1955.

De Bono, E. (1967) *The 5 Day Course in Thinking*. Harmondsworth, Middx: Penguin Books.

Demetriou, A. *et al.* (1999) *Life-Span Developmental Psychology*. West Sussex: John Wiley and Son.

Denzin, N. K. (1995) 'Symbolic Interactionism', in Smith, J. A. *et al.* (eds) *Rethinking Psychology*. London: Sage Publications.

Dulewicz, V. and Higgs, M. (1999) *Emotional Intelligence Questionnaire: User Guide*. Windsor: NFER-Nelson.

Erikson, Eric (1968) *Identity: Youth and Crisis*. New York: Norton.

Eysenck, M. W. and Keane, M. J. (1990) *Cognitive Psychology: A Student's Handbook*. Sussex: Lawrence Erlbaum Associates.

Fanning, Patrick and McKay, Matthew (eds) (2000) *Family Guide to Emotional Wellness: Proven self-help techniques and exercises for dealing with common problems and building crucial life skills*. Oaklands, California: New Haringer Publications Inc.

Faupel, A. *et al.* (1998) *Anger Management – A Practical Guide*. London: David Fulton Publishers.

Fisher, Roger *et al.* (1991) *Getting to Yes: Negotiating Agreement Without Giving In*. USA: Penguin.

Fontana, David (1995) *Psychology for Teachers*. Basingstoke, Hampshire: Macmillan Press.

Gillibrand, Eileen and Mosley, Jenny (1995) *She Who Dares Wins (A woman's guide to professional and personal success)*. London: Harper Collins.

Goleman, Daniel (1996) *Emotional Intelligence: Why it Can Matter More than IQ*. London: Bloomsbury.

Goleman, Daniel (1998) *Working with Emotional Intelligence*. London: Bloomsbury.

Gottman, John (1997) *The Heart of Parenting: How to Raise the Emotionally Intelligent Child*. London: Bloomsbury.

Greenspan, Stanley, I. and Salmon, J. (1993) *First Feelings: Milestones in the Emotional Development of Your Infant and Child from Birth to Age 4*. New York: Viking Press.

Gross, Richard and McIlveen, Rob (1998) *Psychology – A New Introduction*. London: Hodder and Stoughton.

Hansen, Mark Victor and Batten, Joe (1995) *The Master Motivator – Secrets of Inspiring Leadership*. Florida: Health Communications, Inc.

Harrill, Suzanne (1996) *Empowering Teens to Build Self-Esteem*. Houston, Texas: Innerworks Publishing.

Hay McBer (2000) *Research into Teacher Effectiveness: A model of teacher effectiveness*. Research Report No. 216. Norwich: HMSO.

Higgs, M. and Dulewicz, V. (1999) *Making Sense of Emotional Intelligence*. Berkshire: NFER-Nelson Publishing Company.

James, William (1890) *The Principles of Psychology*. New York: Henry Holt.

Kehoe, John (1997) *Mind Power: Into the 21st Century*. Vancouver BC Canada : Zoetic.

Keller, Jeff (1999) *Attitude is Everything*. NY: Inti Publishing and Resource Books.

Lazarus, R. S. (1982) 'Thoughts on the relations between emotion and cognition', *American Psychologist* **37**, 1019–1024.

Lindenfield, Gail (2000) *Super Confidence*. London: Thorsons Publishers.

Loomans, Diane (1994) *Full Esteem Ahead: 100 Ways to Build Self Esteem in Children and Adults*. California, H. J. Kramer.

Mandler, G (1962) 'Emotion', in Brown, R. (ed) *New Directions in Psychology*. New York: Holt, Rhinehart and Winston.

Maslow, A. H. (1968) *Towards a Psychology of Being*. New York: Van Nostrand.

McCarthy, Kevin and Park, James (1998) *Learning by Heart: The Role of Emotional Education in Raising School Achievement*. London: Calouste Gulbenkian Foundation.

McCarthy, Kevin, *Re:membering Education*, 66 Beaconsfield Villas, Brighton, BN1 6HE Tel/Fax: 01273 239311 e-mail: remember@mcmail.com website: www remember.mcmail.com

McNally, David (1993) *Even Eagles Need a Push – Learning to Soar in a Changing World*. London: Thorsons of Harper Collins.

Mental Health and Adolescents in Great Britain (2000) London: Stationery Office.

Montemayor, R. (1983) 'Parents and adolescents in conflict: All families some of the time and some families all of the time', *Journal of Early Adolescence* **3**, 83–103.

Morris, Estelle (1997) SCAA Primary Curriculum Conference (1997) in *The Antidote: Realising the Potential. Emotional Education for All*. An Antidote Report 1996.

Mortimore, P. *et al*. (1988) *School Matters. The Junior Years*. London: Open Books.

National Commission on Education (1996) *Success Against the Odds: Effective Schools in Disadvantaged Areas*. London and New York: Paul Hamlyn Foundation/Routledge.

Orbach, Susie (1998) 'Emotional Literacy', in *Young Minds Magazine*, Mar/Apr **33**, 12–13.

Park, James (Director of Antidote: The Campaign for Emotional Literacy) Unpublished paper presented at South of England Psychology Services Conference December 1999.

Reynolds, D. and Cuttance, P. (eds) (1992) *School Effectiveness: Research, Policy and Practice*. London: Cassell.

Rutter, M. *et al*. (1979) *Fifteen Thousand Hours: Secondary Schools and their effects on Children*. London: Open Books.

Salovey, Peter and Mayer, John, D. (1990) *Emotional Intelligence, Imagination, Cognition and Personality* **9**(3), 185.

Schachter, S. (1964) 'The interaction of cognitive and physiological determinants of emotional state', in Berkowitz, L. (ed) *Advances in Experimental Social Psychology*, Vol. 1. New York: Academic Press.

Schwartz, G. E. *et al.* (1981) 'Cardiovascular differentiation of happiness, sadness, anger, and fear following imagery and exercise', *Psychosomatic Medicine* **43**, 343–364.

Sharp, Peter (2000) 'Promoting Emotional Literacy: Emotional Literacy Improves and Increases Your Life Chances', *Pastoral Care in Education* **18**(3). September (The Journal of the National Association for Pastoral Care in Education). Oxford: Blackwell Publishers.

Sharp, Peter and Herrick, Elizabeth (2000) Promoting Emotional Literacy: Anger Management Groups in Clinical Counselling in Schools, ed. Nick Barwick (2000). London: Routledge.

Sheehy, Gail (1993) 'Pathfinders', in McNally, David *Even Eagles Need a Push*. London: Thorsons.

Sonuga-Barke, E. and Stratford, R. (November 2000) Emotional Literacy in Southampton: Phase One – An Evaluation Report (unpublished). Funded by Calouste Gulbenkian Foundation.

Stein, Steven, J. and Book, Howard, E. (2000) *The EQ Edge: Emotional Intelligence and your Success*. Toronto, Canada: Stoddart Publishing.

Steiner, C. and Perry, P. (1997) *Achieving Emotional Literacy - a personal programme to increase your emotional intelligence*. New York: Avon Books.

TES (2000) *Times Educational Supplement* (27 October).

The Self-Esteem Network, Self-Esteem Directory, 32 Carisbrooke Road, London E17 7EF.

Thorndike, E. L. (p.421) in Nash, J. (1973) *Developmental Psychology: A Psychological Approach*. London: Prentice-Hall.

Watkins, Chris (2000) 'Developing Emotional Intelligence', in *Competency and Emotional Intelligence* **7**(3). London: IRS, Eclipse Group.

Weisenger, Hendrie (1998) *Emotional Intelligence at Work*. San Francisco: Jossey-Bass.

Whyte, David (2000) Unpublished presentation: 'Through the Eye of the Needle: Life, Work and the Poetic Imagination' at Emotional Intelligence Summit, Commonwealth Institute, London (16 May).

Wolf, S. and Wolff, H. G. (1947) *Human Gastric Function*. New York: Oxford University Press.

Woodhead, Chris (1999) *HMI Chief Inspector's Report 1999*. London: OFSTED.

Index